Charles Wood

Beginning life

A series of sermons to the young

Charles Wood

Beginning life
A series of sermons to the young

ISBN/EAN: 9783337264727

Printed in Europe, USA, Canada, Australia, Japan

Cover: Foto ©Lupo / pixelio.de

More available books at **www.hansebooks.com**

BEGINNING LIFE.

A SERIES OF SERMONS TO THE YOUNG.

BY

THE REV. CHARLES WOOD, D. D.

———•———

PHILADELPHIA:
PRESBYTERIAN BOARD OF PUBLICATION
AND SABBATH-SCHOOL WORK,
No. 1334 CHESTNUT STREET.

WESTCOTT & THOMSON,
Stereotypers and Electrotypers, Philada.

DEDICATED

TO THE

YOUNG PEOPLE'S SOCIETY

OF

CHRISTIAN ENDEAVOR

OF THE

FIRST PRESBYTERIAN CHURCH,

GERMANTOWN, PHILADELPHIA,

AND TO ALL THE YOUNG PEOPLE OF THAT CHURCH
AND CONGREGATION.

CONTENTS.

I.
Is Life a Career, or a Mission? . . . . PAGE 7

II.
Youth 23

III.
Friendships 33

IV.
What shall we Read? 49

V.
The Forming of Habits 65

VI.
Perpetual Youth 83

VII.
Temptation 97

VIII.

Making a Home 113

IX.

Strength 129

X.

Success 145

I.
IS LIFE A CAREER, OR A MISSION?

BEGINNING LIFE.

I.

IS LIFE A CAREER, OR A MISSION?

"I must work the works of Him that sent me, while it is day."—JOHN ix. 4.

THE life of Jesus Christ was pervaded with a feeling of responsibility. He spoke of himself as having come to this earth on a most momentous mission, and his thoughts were perpetually concentrated upon the accomplishment of it. They who have entered most fully into the meaning of his life have had some such feeling about themselves. His mission was infinitely more glorious than theirs, or than that of any human being, but all his brethren, as he calls us, must have, like him, a God-given work to do. This, it must be confessed, is a somewhat serious, not to say sombre, view to take of life; it is a view that theoretically very many, and practically very many more, openly or tacitly refuse to take. Life, as they look at it, is a career—something to be played like a game; and he who wins, though he may have broken all the rules, is to have the prize.

This is the popular view that is spreading like a contagion, and no land is more exposed than our own. We have no hereditary rulers; our ancestors preserved us from ever waiting "as sycophants in the court of kings;" but we satisfy the servile part of our natures by the abject homage we pay success. The smart man, the man who gets on, who does what he sets out to do in whatever way, is getting to be our national hero. Hereditary position and wealth count for less here than in England, but the self-made man, the man who lifts himself above his fellows and wrings a fortune from the hands of reluctant Fate, is the one before whom Liberty herself would uncap if her helmet were not riveted to her beautiful head.

I shall make no effort at this time to overturn this theory by weight of argument; I shall rather attempt to displace it by causing some of the figures most prominent in the English-speaking world to pass before you, and as you see that they have each broken away from or outgrown the conception of life as a career, you may come to see as they saw that life is a mission. I am encouraged in this attempt by the fact that this audience is so largely made up of the young, for, as the rabbis say, "to teach wisdom to the old is to write it in water; to teach it to the young is to grave it on stone."

Let me hold before you, first, as a sort of background for my dissolving-views, the form of one who never rose above the conception of life as a career, and who would have been, if that definition were correct, a most brilliant success. Eleven years ago, in the vestibule of the English House of Commons, I saw a man of sphinx-like face gazing, with a score or more dignified companions, at a statue of some famous statesman that had just been put in place. This man at whom we were looking was at that time on the crest of the wave; a man of fashion, a writer of sensational melodramatic novels, a member of Parliament hissed back into his seat after his first speech, the leader of his party, the prime minister of the realm, an earl, and is still, a decade after his death, a popular idol; and, withal, a Hebrew. No such phenomenon had ever before appeared in English history. He was a nimble matador, fastening his darts in the necks of his enraged adversaries as they rushed upon him while he stepped aside with a light laugh, half at them and half at himself. This winner of all the honors must have died a disappointed man, for it is doing him no injustice, if one may judge from all that he ever said or did, to say that he lived for power and thought the man either a fool or a hypocrite who professed any less earthly motive; and power was the one thing that he lost before his death. He was no longer prime minister: his hated rival had the rank that was heaven to him. Life as a career even the marvelous Hebrew would probably have pronounced a failure.

Compare this life with that of another English earl covering almost the same decades. No high office was his, but he was an enthusiast in doing good. There was scarcely a society, philanthropic or Christian, in all London that could not count on his support. All the downtrodden and oppressed felt that he was their friend. Multitudes are living happier, nobler lives to-day because of Shaftesbury. Where is there one nobly inspired by the brilliant statesman, the unrivaled organizer of dramatic international councils?

Standing only a few feet away from the Hebrew earl that afternoon in the vestibule of the House of Commons was a man of a very different type. He was then supposed to be suffering from the defeat that had carried himself and his party out of power, but his influence had never been greater, and the real work of his life was being carried on as quietly and as successfully as if those adverse votes had never been cast. Even as a boy he was so remarkable, both intellectually and morally, that a young Eaton lad now famous as the late dean of the Abbey was taken to see him as a reward for well-doing. He grew steadily upon the world till by almost common consent among his kin beyond the sea he is known as the greatest of living Englishmen. He too, like the Hebrew earl, has held his honors lightly, though not for the same reasons. He has gone from cabinet meetings where the destiny of a continent was decided, to pray with some dying laborer on his estate. He has probably accepted gladly the great offices to which he has been called, but he has never forgotten that his real mission here, like that of every other true man, is to work the works of Him that sent him. The success of both these lives is beyond us, but not the eagerness for it of the one or the comparative indifference to it of the other. The fidelity to a high ideal that makes one of these lives so admirable is not beyond the reach of the very humblest.

Not unworthy to be mentioned in the same breath with the great statesman and the Christian apologist is the gray-haired, silver-tongued orator of the Society of Friends. Perhaps he was the truest and most hopeful friend we had in England during our war. He looked across the sea in the dark hour when Northern armies were thrown back broken and discouraged, and through the smoke of the conflict he saw the glowing vision of "one vast confederation stretching in an unbroken line from the frozen North to the glowing South and from the wild billows of the Atlantic westward to the calmer waters of the Pacific main; and I see," said he, "one people and one language and one law and one faith over all that wide continent, the home of freedom and the refuge of the oppressed of every land and of every clime." On the morning of the first day of each week he takes his place with a little company in sombre garb whose worship of God is mostly of the silent sort, but his, at least, is so sincere that more than once he has followed his convictions concerning war and peace, out of office into obscurity as great as is possible for such a man. It has been altogether impossible for him to accept any position, however honorable, that would hinder his doing as he understands it "the works of Him that sent him."

"If I could choose my lot in life," said one idler to another, "I would be an English duke." The possibilities open to one born in that position are somewhat dazzling. Apparently, such a one has only to close his fingers upon the prizes that fall unsought into his palms. Like one of our rich men's sons, who has no need to do anything if he has no wish to be anything but a rich man's son, he has no need to exert himself if he does not wish to be anything but a duke. But even men who have inherited a career so brilliant have not ignobly contented themselves with it, but have felt that they too were called to work the works of Him that sent them into the ducal palace. There is a duke allied by marriage to the English queen upon whom I ask you to look, not because of the splendor of his rank or of the glory reflected from the crown, but because his view of life is that of a responsible mission which it has been his purpose to accomplish in a way pleasing to his Master. No small portion of his life has been devoted to diligent study of nature and of law. No better exposition of the reign of Law has been given than his. Convinced of the unseen Presence everywhere, it has been his effort to show how

> "The whole round earth is every way
> Bound by gold chains about the feet of God."

The qualities which make him most admirable, his fidelity, his devotion to duty and truth, are within the reach of the humblest mechanic and clerk. The virtues which shine so brightly to men's eyes when they are exhibited by those of exalted rank shine as brightly in God's eyes when set in the most lowly surroundings. The same "Well done!" is to be spoken at last to all good and faithful servants, whether they come from the hills or from the valleys of earth.

It is openly asserted that Christianity has lost its grip on the thinking men of these modern times. An English poet who gives voice to many thoughts that are in the air depicts this age as one of transition. He finds himself, he says,

> "Wandering between two worlds,
> One dead, the other powerless to be born."

The leaders of thought are dumb; they have no fair visions to which to point; they have no high calls to go in and possess the land of promise lying within sight.

> "Achilles ponders in his tent;
> The kings of modern thought are dumb:
> Silent they are, though not content,
> And wait to see the future come—
> Silent while years engrave the brow.
> Silent! the best are silent now."

But I see an old man who has long swayed the destinies of England rising in his place in the House of Commons, and in the great hush that comes upon that assembly and the whole English-speaking world when he speaks, I hear him say, "I believe in God the Father Almighty, Maker of heaven and earth, and in Jesus Christ, his only Son, our Lord." By his side stands the silver-tongued orator of England, and with him are the scientific duke and the poet-laureate and the most thoughtful of all the poets of our time, and they too repeat their creed: "We believe in God the Father Almighty, Maker of heaven and earth, and in Jesus Christ, his only Son, our Lord." Ah, no! The best are not all silent now.

Life may be a meaningless career, as it has been, and is, to vast multitudes; it may be a most significant and exalted mission. It is very much what we make of it. It is told of a witty dean that, arriving somewhat prematurely one evening at a reception, he was the first to enter the great drawing-room hung on every side with mirrors, and, seeing his own form reflected everywhere, he rubbed his hands and said, "Ah! a gathering of the clergy, I see!" So men come into life where there are great reflectors on every side. The avaricious man rubs his hands and says, "Ah! a gathering of money-getters, I see!" The ambitious man rubs his hands and says, "Ah! a gathering of place-hunters, I see!" The lotus-eater rubs his hands and says, "Ah! a gathering of pleasure-seekers, I see!" and the cynic rubs his hands and says, "Ah! a gathering of apes, I see, making faces at one another!" while the true-hearted man rubs his hands and says, "Ah! a gathering of men, I see!" As Lowell says,

> "Be noble, and the nobleness that lies
> Sleeping in other men, but never dead,
> Will rise in majesty to meet thine own."

Let life be for you a high and holy embassy, and you will find multitudes as eager as yourself to work the works of Him that sent them.

There are but two essentials for a truly successful life. The first of these is nobleness of ideal. Follow anything but the highest and best, and your work will be needlessly faulty. High above the fair city on the Arno, near the church of San Miniato, stands Michael Angelo's statue of David. To the untrained eye it is one of his masterpieces, but artists tell us it is the least perfect of anything he has left us. The story is that Angelo in an unfortunate moment accepted the partly-executed design of another, of course inferior, sculptor, and, though possessed of almost more than human skill, he was never able to overcome those faults that could only have been escaped by destroying utterly the imperfect design. Accept any merely human model as your ideal of the perfect life, and you will never attain to that which was possible to you; accept the perfect man Christ Jesus as the ideal toward which you wish to work and into which you wish your life to come, and nothing can prevent your success. You shall be satisfied at last, for you shall be transformed into that likeness. The work of each day will fit easily into the great purposes of your life; you will have no desire to escape from your present lot into another more advantageous, but your desire will be to do what you have to do unto his glory. You will see how true it is, as Herbert says,

> "All may of Thee partake;
> Nothing can be so mean
> That with this tincture, 'For thy sake,'
> Will not grow fair and clean.
>
> "A servant with this clause
> Makes drudgery divine;
> Who sweeps a room as to thy laws
> Makes that and th' action fine."

The moment Christ becomes your ideal you will hear him teaching you that to be his disciple it is not necessary to do singular things: it is only necessary "to do common things singularly well."

The second essential to make this mission we call life a successful one is steadfastness of purpose. Conquerors are men who have given and taken hard blows. On their knees in the dust one moment, before their adversary can cry "Surrender!" they are up again and ready to charge. General Grant used to say there was a time in every hard-fought battle when both sides were beaten; the commander who strikes the first hard blow after that wins the battle. The man who is easily discouraged, who believes the first person who says, "You'll never amount to anything," and either gets out of the fight altogether or gives only half-hearted blows, certainly never will amount to very much. But the man who is determined, who expects to get a good many hard knocks and some severe wounds, and who knows how to die, but not how to retreat or surrender, is sure in the end to win if he is fighting on the right side—on God's side. Are you down now? Are you out of work? Are you thoroughly discouraged? Don't give up! I saw a list the other day of our most successful business-men, and in almost every instance you had only to go back ten, fifteen or twenty years to find these very men, now on the crest of the wave, in the trough of the sea. They wouldn't be beaten, and so they couldn't be.

> "The heights by great men reached and kept
> Were not attained by sudden flight,
> But they, while their companions slept,
> Were toiling upward in the night."

Have no fear of the night. Christ, your Brother, waits for you there in the darkness, and he will lead you, if you trust him, safe through to the light beyond. Let your ideal of life be that of a high and holy mission. Set yourself determinedly to work the works of Him who sent you, wheresoever you are and in the midst of whatever discouragements, and it needs even now no prophet to write your epitaph. The world may never think you a brilliant success; but when you die, "all nature will rise up and say, This was a man," and those who knew you best will say, "This was a Christian man." And Christ has promised that he will have something to say to such a one that will thrill the soul as all the honors of the court and the camp and the forum never could.

II.
YOUTH.

II.

YOUTH.

"Let no man despise thy youth."—1 TIM. iv. 12.

YOUTH is in danger of having contempt put upon it by those who are young and wish they were older, and those who are old and wish they were younger. They who have it are tempted to underestimate a familiar possession, as they who have it no longer are tempted to belittle that which is for ever beyond their reach. Timothy, like all youthful teachers, was exposed to the possibility of being unappreciated by those of his own age and ignored by those who were no longer young; Timothy himself is in danger of falsely appraising that for which even Paul seems to offer an indirect apology, and of sometimes wishing he were not embarrassed by such riches. Nothing makes a young person blush so quickly as to be charged with youth. Probably every young man wishes himself older as fervently as most old men wish themselves younger. Not till we pass through youth and look back upon it do we see how very far indeed it was from being a despicable epoch in our lives. Youth is like a picture from which we must be removed, a little way, at least—if we would see it properly. "Happy are the young, for they have life before them," we are sure must have been said by a man who was thus removed by the consciousness of swiftly-coming old age.

> "There are gains for all our losses,
>   There are balms for all our pains;
> But when youth, the dream, departs,
> It takes something from our hearts,
>   And it never comes again."

What prodigals we all are in youth! We spend like princes, as if we had royal treasuries to draw from. What spendthrifts we are of time! Our only question concerning it is how we shall pass it most quickly and pleasantly by. A queen proffers her realm for an inch of time, and the youth flings away with a light heart the small coin of days and weeks and the larger pieces of months and years. We laugh at the clock and statistics and preachers when we are young. Nothing seems to us so absurd as the undeniable proofs they give us that after a decade or so of years this youth that we have accustomed ourselves to think of as belonging to us, like our names or our physiognomies, will be ours no longer, and we shall be old then like those people who we think were probably always venerable. We can more easily think of ourselves as wanting anything else than time. Youth has such a way of prolonging years into cycles! Perhaps even the queen who bid so high for that single inch of time was once young, and had, as you have now, more of it at her disposal than she knew what to do with.

What a spendthrift youth is of health! A perennial spring it seems of an inexhaustible supply. Only at dawn and in the early morning the fabled fountain of Ammon overflowed, but this fountain bubbles and leaps and shoots high its waters all the long day of youth. What wonder that like careless servants we should let the waters waste, too indifferent to husband that which we think limitless! What would not the old man give for even a few drops of those waters he scattered in youth! All your wealth then will not seem to you an exorbitant price for that of which you think now as without value. More than Lucullus ever spent on any of his banquets hard-headed business-men stand ready to pay for a single meal of the simplest sort eaten with the appetite of health. They are almost ready to barter any hopes they may have had of a paradise of unending delights for a day of such fresh, keen joy as they had almost too many of in their youth.

What a spendthrift youth is of hope! Its exaggerated vision brings everything easily within the range of the possible. All these graduates who will emerge this spring from our twelve universities and three hundred and thirty-three colleges know just how to set the rivers on fire; and if it is worth while, they will do it. They will put right the times that are out of joint. The world has waited for them with surprising and commendable patience, but the world shall find that it did well in waiting. "Youth faces the sun, and all the shadows fall behind out of sight." Why croak about them? Why not forget that there are any shadows? Alas that even such apparently inexhaustible treasures should at last fail—that they who once saw everything rose-tinted should come at last to see everything in a cold hard light whose rays are like javelins stabbing every hope dead at the moment of its birth!

What a spendthrift, too, youth is of opportunities! They are so bewilderingly abundant! Any effort to seize them is like plucking flowers in an interminable garden. There are beds everywhere as far as the eye can reach, and each bed seems more beautiful than the other. Why stop here rather than there? Just as the hand is about to gather one the eye catches a glimpse of another more exquisite still. So at last with empty hands the exit is reached. They are very young indeed who do not look back already to other days when there were many things that might have been could they but have brought themselves to take the opportunity that was offered, but it seemed so improbable that other opportunities still more desirable would not, and that very soon, come within reach, that for the most part they were allowed to slip by, often without any recognition whatever.

"Ah! five and twenty years ago
Had I but planted seeds of trees,

> How now I should enjoy their
> Shade, and see their fruit
> Swing in the breeze!"

Most fortunate man was that poet if he had nothing more serious to lament than that. There are very few whose memory takes them back even half the five and twenty years who cannot see many places where, through neglect on their part, much sadder mistakes were made. "Had we," they say, "but studied in school or in college, what an education we might have had! Being educated, what might we not have accomplished! Had we been industrious in that first position we got in the store, we might have stayed there to this day, and been promoted as rapidly as some we know. Had we resisted this appetite that now cries with loud voice almost ceaselessly for gratification, it might long ago have been quieted or hushed altogether. Had we but begun at this or that epoch to live as we feel now, and as we felt then we ought to live, by this time a good life, an open, aggressive Christian life, would have become almost a second nature to us, and the agonies through which, as we imagine, at least, we must now pass before we can enter on such a life would have been avoided altogether."

Youth is rich, too, in fancy. There are no colors on the painter's palette like those with which youth transforms this sombre world. It is optimistic, or should be. It has high aspirations and no doubts of their realization. It is a time of impressions—of first impressions. The world is all new. Its joys and its sorrows alike come with the dew on them. A word, a gesture, a look, are photographed on the sensitized plate that youth keeps always exposed, and half a century hence the lines made in that minute fragment of a moment will still be as clear as on the first day. There are impressions traced long ago on your soul that you would willingly erase. You can forget many things with only too great ease. The book you read, the scenes you saw, the conversation you heard, yesterday, are already gliding into that mist that swarms with dim and vanishing outlines; but the book you read, the scenes you saw, the conversation you heard, twenty or fifty years ago are as distinct as if but an hour had passed. The same events could not cut themselves as deeply now into your memory. The material has hardened. It is crossed and recrossed with lines, and the cut must be very sharp and deep indeed to stand out clear and distinct now after many days. It goes without saying that youth is the time when one should most hesitate to expose one's self to undesirable impressions.

Youth is as impulsive as it is impressionable. "The heart controls in youth; in manhood the head takes the lead." It would be sad for the world if the epoch of impulse were altogether omitted. There would be few mistakes certainly if we were all born into that period where the head takes the lead, but there would as certainly be few heroic deeds that send the blood rushing with almost dangerous rapidity through the veins, and that give even the dull-eyed a glimpse of "the far-off land of beauty and of goodness." It is to the young the world looks to have her cold old heart warmed now and then by some chivalric act, by some splendid exhibition of valor and of self-sacrifice. It is to the young, an old man says, the world must look for even intellectual quickening. "New ideas build their nests," he says, "in young brains." "Revolutions are not made by men in spectacles, and the whisperings of new truths are not caught by those who begin to feel the need of an ear-trumpet." The outward change, the dimmed eye, the wrinkled, colorless cheek, the trembling hand, have ordinarily their counterpart within. Neither heart nor brain can escape the shriveling touch of old age. As we grow old we become stolid, and it is scarcely worth while for a great thought or a fine impulse to visit us then for the first time and run the risk of being refused admission as a stranger or of being turned out ignominiously as a disturber of the peace. No man in England over forty years of age, it is said, could be persuaded at the time it was made that Harvey's discovery of the circulation of the blood was anything but a plausible theory of an ignorant quack calculated to deceive only the superficially educated. "New ideas build their nests in young brains."

Youth is the age of faith—of credulity, if you

please. No Munchausen tale can be too marvelous for its digestion. The wonders of the Arabian Nights are not half wonderful enough for its appetite. It has no experience from which to build a conception of the ordinary or the possible. It must, therefore, believe what it hears and reads. Every man is received at his own appraisement by the young. If he claims to know everything and to be able to do anything, youth has no inclination or reason for disputing his most colossal assumptions. A difference of six months in age, of an inch in stature, is sufficient to make a hero of the older and larger boy for the younger and smaller. Kings do not so overwhelm us in middle life as the big boy in youth. Every child's father is the strongest and wisest and best man in all the world, from whose hand it is almost as easy to take a creed as to take an apple. The most stupendous statements are swallowed with nearly as great ease as is the most luscious fruit. Fathers who believe anything themselves are criminally careless if they do not make wise use of this receptive period to write their own faith indelibly on the child's heart.

Youth is like a fair unwalled city open to the enemy on every side. Its very virtues are like ornamented terraces, concealing enemies in their approach and serving, when skillfully used by an adroit foe, as breastworks affording the most complete protection from the missiles of the beleaguered. With what satanic ingenuity has each of those qualities that make youth most attractive been used to accomplish its ruin!

But youth is by no means an unmixed aggregation of virtues. It has weaknesses somewhat peculiar to itself, as well as numerous others that are the common inheritance of humanity at every epoch. Curiosity, while not confined to youth, is supposed to be most vigorous then. Pandora was very young when her curiosity got the better of her and she lifted the lid of the forbidden jar and filled the world, the legend says, with all the ills that trouble men and make them sometimes doubt whether life is worth living. It is in youth that we are most tempted to follow Pandora's example and fill our lives with evils that can never be gathered up again and thrust back into the jar whose lid should not have been disturbed. Where is the man who as a boy was content till he had made himself half sick with a cigar, or had burnt his tongue with fire-water, or had defiled his lips with an oath, "just to see how it would seem" to do those things that he saw other half-grown boys and men doing? "You ought to try it and see what it's like" is the commonest, and not infrequently the most effective, form of temptation with which youth is allured into the paths whose end is disappointment and pain and death.

There are stronger desires as well that are not satisfied with a sip and a taste. Neither are these coarse appetites frightened into silence when the air is filled with flying terrors that should never have been let loose. The most destructive exhibition of passion in the world's history has been by young men. Paris was young when to gratify a whim he plunged Greece and Troy into a merciless war. Antony was young when he sacrificed an empire for a few days of sensuous joy. Napoleon was young when he shook every throne and laid every capital of Europe under tribute to gratify his insatiable ambition. Even Renan warned the students of Paris the other day not to let the strong desires of youth raise up for them ghosts to fill the air with their maledictions.

Youth should be—*must* be—the time of decision. You are the prize, young men and maidens, for which hosts contend. The aged for the most part are already apportioned, but both Folly and Wisdom lift up their voices and plead with you. You cannot be long undecided. You will consent to be led in the mad dance of death or straight forward on paths of pleasantness and peace. This is a time of would-be procrastination. You wish to wait. You are trying to conjugate every verb in the future. You like to say what you will do after a few months or years. But God is pressing you by every high and holy motive to make your decision now for truth and righteousness and Christ. Then you will be a divinely-directed soul, and the promise of youth shall be fulfilled in a useful manhood, an honored old age and an eternity of unspeakable joy.

III.
FRIENDSHIPS.

III.

FRIENDSHIPS.

"A man that hath friends must show himself friendly; and there is a Friend that sticketh closer than a brother."—Prov. xviii. 24.

THERE are cold-blooded batrachian creatures who have no desire for friends. "We can do very well," they say, "without any such sickly sentimentality as that form of selfishness that masks itself under the romantic guise of friendship. It is well enough for very young people," they sneer, "to swear eternal fealty to one another in an oath that may be sacredly kept till the crescent moon that witnessed it becomes a completely rounded circle, but men who have cut their wisdom-teeth see that that sort of thing is dangerous business."

When you let outsiders get too far into your life, you have put yourself in their hands and you are at their mercy. You have doubled the complications and cares of life. You must look out now not only for yourself, but for that much-less-to-be-trusted second self who may unmake you by an unthinking admission or a designed disclosure. The best of friends are broken reeds that are bound sooner or later to pierce the hand that leans upon them, and friends of the average sort are like sand between the teeth; the sooner you get rid of them, the better.

This is a very uninviting account to give of a relation about which so many fine things have been said, but the men who give it us are not ordinarily particularly fine men. They talk as Guy Fawkes and his accomplices might have done; and if their great purpose in life resembles in any way that of Fawkes, they are justified in being as chary as he of friendships and confidences. The young rarely suffer from such aggravated attacks of misanthropy. A young person's heart is said to be "like a child's mouth, into which everything is put." They are as eager for friendships as for candies and cakes and ices, and are as ready in one case as the other to accept very poor imitations in place of the pure article. They do not always know the difference. Did not your father and mine understand this? Else why did they warn us, when we went to the school or the college or the store, to make haste slowly in our friendships? They may have forgotten that Shakespeare ever said,

> "But do not dull thy palm with entertainment
> Of each new-hatched, unfledged comrade."

They may not even have had in mind the warnings Solomon sprinkled thick amongst his proverbs for those who have clasped hands and exchanged vows with strangers; they were speaking altogether from observation and experience, but that did not make their words any less pointed and weighty.

That we did not take their warnings as much to heart as we might have done was natural too: our pride was a little hurt that it was thought possible for us to be so easily deceived as to make such warnings necessary. It was hurt a little more at the insinuation that our friendship was not such a sufficient prize in itself as to make it necessary to suggest some ulterior motive in the professed seekers of it. And when the warning was directed toward friends we had already made, it took on a still less attractive form. How unkind it seemed to arouse suspicion of one so fair of face and form and speech and manner, so witty and wise, as our dearest friend! How unfair to presume that if there was anything wrong we who knew him so well would not have discovered it! What young David Copperfield has ever had a doubt of the Steerforths till suggested, and has not spurned it then? Where are the young men and the young maidens who believe for a moment that the citadel of their lives may be in greatest danger from attacks made under the guise of friendship, and that the great tempter may use their friend as hunters use the decoy elephant to lead his unsuspicious acquaintances, with many a caress of his proboscis, straight to the traps arranged for them? If the elephants were on their guard, they would very quickly detect these frauds; and if you were on your guard, you would very quickly detect these false friends.

There are certain signs that always betray the dangerous applicant for your friendship. One of these signs is frivolity. It does not necessarily follow that because a man has a long face and walks with all the dignity of a stork he is particularly trustworthy. Monkeys steal and play all sorts of mean tricks with very grave countenances, but the creature, man or woman, that is always laughing, that giggles in the school, on the street and in the church, and considers no fact in life of any significance that cannot easily be giggled over, is a mere clown to whom the world is a great circus, and the giggling you hear is only the tinkling of the bells in the fool's cap. Wit and humor are most estimable, most desirable. They act like springs. While they do not smooth the road more or less hard we all must travel, they ease the bumps and jolts most pleasantly. The man who can make others laugh a clear, ringing laugh with no Schuylkill-like mud in it prevents many a visit from the family doctor, the man who can laugh such a laugh himself may be most of the time his own physician; but perpetual cachinnation is the laughter of fools, that to Solomon's wise ear sounded like "the crackling of thorns under the pot." There is no depth, no seriousness, in such a nature. Beware of these gigglers as sailors beware of waters that break with every breeze into white-caps and foam. There are shallows, quicksands, perhaps, under those pretty waves.

Another sign that should warn you that your would-be friend must prove a dangerous companion is cynicism. He smiles often, this candidate for favor, but there is no spontaneity to it. It sounds more like a hiss than like a laugh as it comes from his half-closed teeth. His lip curls constantly at mention of things you were taught to reverence. He sneers at all the "old worn-out ideas," so he calls them, of industry and honesty, of virtue and religion. He makes his mock at the Church and at the Sunday-school, and wonders that a person of your good sense can countenance such instruments of superstition. He more than hints that only children pray and only old women and weak-minded men read their Bibles. It was such friends that laughed one of the strongest-winged poets of England out of the faith of his early manhood and left him to die without hope, a stranger in a strange land. Such friends will sneer away your belief both in God and in man. They will cover with ice all the one-time warm springs of feeling and emotion. They will bring you to classify men of every sort as simply as they have done into the two categories of the "openly bad and the secretly bad." They will take away your heart of flesh, and will give you a mere muscle like their own, whose only function is to keep up the circulation. They will steal away the weapons with which you once guarded your treasures, and then they will steal these treasures themselves, persuading you, at the same time, that they all, purity, truth, honor, virtue, goodness, God or man's, have no existence except in the diseased imagination. They will leave you, like a disarmed, dismantled and stranded ship-of-war on some unknown coast, with nothing to fight with or for. Beware of such friends.

Another warning sign of danger from a would-be friend is dissimulation. He comes, this candidate for favor, with no ceaseless laugh of frivolity or perpetual sneer of cynicism, for his finger is upon his lips, as if detectives were on his track and as if silence were his only hope. He whispers the commonest facts into your ear as if they were dead secrets. He has unutterable things to tell you which he will communicate only on your pledge never to breathe them to any one, especially to your parents and your teachers. Only rely upon him, and he assures you of his readiness to show you how to enjoy every forbidden pleasure without running any risk of committing the unpardonable sin of being found out. All his pockets are filled with a peculiar kind of very fine dust, which he throws into too watchful eyes with the greatest skill. These "friends" are in every school, in both the boys' and the girls' departments, always ready to give unpaid instruction in the art of breaking rules without being caught. They teach the boys how to get cigarettes and illustrated newspapers, and the girls how to get forbidden sweets and yellow-backed novels, without such old fogies as parents and teachers being any the wiser. They will show these same pupils of theirs, as they become a little more apt, how to go to the theatres and to visit dance-halls without arousing suspicion in the unsympathetic hearts of their aged guardians. These dissimulators will be as false to you as they are false to the old folks whom they are teaching you to outwit. They are false to you now. They are giving you false and fatal ideas of life and happiness; and when these ideas have resulted in your ruin, as unhindered they inevitably will, the dissimulator, too astute to be caught himself, will stand aside and laugh at you for going so far down the path along which his own hand pushed you.

Still another dangerous sign in an acquaintance who desires promotion to friendship is extravagance. It shows itself, probably, at first, only in speech. Every sentence is overloaded with adjectives. As the spendthrift handles nothing but gold or silver, so your would-be friend deals in no smaller coin than superlatives and comparatives. He sees everything on an exaggerated scale. If it were not that his pulse is normal, you would easily believe him to be breathing pure oxygen all the time. By just so much as he exaggerates himself and his ways he belittles you and yours. He makes you ashamed of your home: it is so unassuming. He calls it "inadequate" for such a person as you, by a little instruction from him, would soon become. He makes you ashamed of your old father and mother. He is very careful not to say so in words, but he makes you feel that they are hardly such progenitors as you might have been expected to have. Under his influence your manner toward them changes: it becomes less deferential, not to say less respectful. You feel as you never did before that they are by no means necessary to your happiness, and that they might easily become hindrances to it. He makes you ashamed of your work. You were ready to have every one congratulate you like a cabinet-officer six months ago, when you got a place in the mill or the store or on the railroad; but that was before you had met this friend. He isn't doing much himself, perhaps nothing at all just at present, but he makes the impression on you that there are very few pairs of shoes anywhere much too large for him to step into whenever he chooses. You have only to talk with him a few minutes at any time to have all the zest taken out of your work. You go back to the spindles or the counter or the office with a dull, heavy sense in your heart that all this is beneath you, that you ought to be an employer instead of being an employé, a wholesale instead of a retail dealer, a leader in society instead of a director or a directress of the formless thoughts of very young people and little children to uninteresting and stupid subjects. His touch has the same effect upon your income as upon your work: it shrinks into itself as some sensitive things do when rudely handled. You wonder that you were ever satisfied with it as you see it now in the light he has thrown upon it. Why should you exert such abilities as he assures you you possess—and you have long suspected it—for such an insignificant remuneration? "Almost better to take nothing at all than so little," you say, and he says, "Quite right; now you talk like yourself." So you give up the position that has become too small for your enlarged self-conceit, and look around for something really first class, something that will be worthy of your hitherto unrecognized abilities. While you are looking you find some things for which you were not on the lookout. You find that you can't live comfortably on big words, even inflated so perfectly as your friend's words are; that the coat you thought too shabby to wear when you gave up work is steadily gaining only in lightness of weight and in increased reflective power; that the appraisement you had set upon yourself is suffering, in spite of your indignation that it should be so, by the lack of demand for your valuable services.

But your friend does not desert you. He reveals

to you the fact that there are many ways of living well without going through the commonplace routine of what is called "making a living." He explains to you how feasible some of these are. It is an opportune moment for the tempter, such a moment as Jacob took to show Esau how he might have a good meal of savory pottage without getting it for himself; so opportune that you too, like Esau, sell your birthright as a son of God, as an heir, through Christ, of heaven, for the thing now within your reach that you want so very much.

Or your extravagant friend, while he says nothing about your work or your income from it, gives his attention to your recreations and amusements. They have always been of the simplest and least expensive kind. You were brought up to think first of how much cloth you had, and then of how to cut the pattern to fit it; but your friend soon convinces you that this is a very plebeian method indeed. There are certain forms of enjoying one's self that are entirely respectable and appropriate. Others may be cheaper, but they are impossible except to those who are so far below public opinion as to be indifferent to it. That these are expensive is unfortunately true, but this is no reason why you should deny yourself of them. Your whole style of living is gradually changed to suit these new pleasures, and, while your income remains the same, your expenses have been doubled. There can be nothing before you but bankruptcy or Canada; and Canada is bankruptcy.

But you will reform this extravagant friend of yours. He is, you confess, somewhat too fast now. He will undoubtedly be ruined financially, socially, morally, if he cannot be checked in his impetuous downward course, but who so well adapted to put on the brakes as yourself? You are willing to be his friend. You are sympathetic; you understand him. You go part-way with him, and therefore he will be most likely to halt when you give the sign, and retrace his steps under your direction. You may give the sign if you are not too intoxicated yourself with the delightful rapidity of motion, but he will pay as much attention to it as a runaway horse pays to a child's hand on the rein. If your friend is to be reformed, it will need some one older and firmer than yourself. For you to go part way with him will only mean two lives ruined instead of one.

This capacity for friendship of which we are most of us conscious—does it mean nothing? is it never to be gratified? Are you, who see in each new acquaintance a possible friend—one who shall understand you, who shall make it possible for you to be and express your true best self,—are you to be perpetually disappointed?

If you admit into your life these frivolous, cynical, dissimulating and extravagant friends against whom you have been warned, you will have made the coming of the true friend impossible. A man that hath friends is a man who has shown himself friendly. He has exhibited such qualities as attract real, true friends, more reliable, even, than blood-relations. Jonathan never would have given his friendship, one of the purest and noblest in the world's history, to David if David had not been the man he was. It was because Damon was worthy of Pythias, and Pythias worthy of Damon, that each thought it a privilege to die for the other. The slightest shadow of insincerity, of self-seeking, in either would have acted upon their friendship as an insulating substance acts upon an electric magnet. The two hearts held so tightly together by the mysterious current flowing through them, that even death could not tear them asunder, would have fallen instantly apart like two bars of iron suddenly demagnetized.

For a true friend any sacrifice of pride, of ambition, of ease, comfort, is worth making. He cannot be kept without a willingness to make such a sacrifice should it be needed. For a true friend even the sacrifice of his friendship is worth making if the occasion calls for it. Sir Walter Raleigh thought this the final test. "Thou mayest be sure," he says, "that he that will in private tell thee of thy faults is thy friend; for he adventures thy dislike and doth hazard thy hatred." If done in the right spirit, your friend is giving you the highest possible proof of his friendship when he opens your eyes to see some fault or weakness that might very easily, if undiscovered, prove fatal. "Faithful are the wounds of a friend." There are none so painful, none that cut so deep, but they are clean and healthy and ought to heal rapidly. "Better be a nettle in the side of your friend than his echo."

The friend such as we desire Emerson thinks is a dream and a fable. The friend who is perfectly true and perfectly tender, and who understands us as we do not understand ourselves, is to be found only in ideal descriptions; and Emerson is right if we confine our search unnecessarily, as he seems to have done. He tells us of the world's great heroes and seems to have fathomed their virtues and vices, but he has very little, if anything, to tell us of a certain Judean Teacher whose character has now been scrutinized with extremest care for two thousand years without the discovery of a single blot. Why will not this Man from Nazareth serve as the ideal friend? He was perfectly true and perfectly tender, and he constantly showed that he knew more of men than they knew of themselves. Why cannot the Goethes and Voltaires and Rénans and Emersons take him for their friend if they will not take him as their Saviour? By their own confession he was all they seek or could desire. They posed before the world as philosophers, but has he a right to be called a lover of wisdom who when he acknowledgedly sees what he professes to seek refuses to receive it? We do not call ourselves philosophers, but we may easily be more philosophical than they. The ideal friend is not to appear in some distant golden age: he has appeared. He seeks us because we have need of him. He asks us to be enrolled amongst the number of his friends. "Ye have not chosen me," he says, "but I have chosen you." The conditions for becoming and remaining his friend are of the simplest sort: "Ye are my friends if ye do whatsoever I command you;" and his commands are not impossible or unreasonable. We are to love one another, to be kind and forgiving and helpful. We are to do right ourselves, and to assist every one else, as far as we can, to do right. This is all, and in return he will befriend us always. He will give us the use of his name. He will lend us his strength as we struggle with our appetites and our sins. He will hold our hands when we stumble; and when we come to the river from the touch of whose waters we all shrink, his grasp will tighten when the grasp of other hands that have tenderly pressed our own is no longer felt. He will be with us in the new life that opens beyond, and will be our constant guide and instructor till the home-feeling comes to us. Why should you live a day longer without this Friend? "I do not wonder," says Ruskin, "at what men suffer; I do wonder at what they lose."

IV.
WHAT SHALL WE READ?

IV.

WHAT SHALL WE READ?

"Of making many books there is no end: and much study is a weariness of the flesh."—ECCL. xii. 13.

SOLOMON'S lament over the endless number of books in the world would have gained something in intensity and pathos could he have foreseen the public libraries of Berlin, Paris, London, Washington and Philadelphia. He sighed when he looked upon a few hundred carefully-copied manuscripts lying on the shelves of his royal library. "What's the use," he thought, "of so many? No man can read them all." Wise as the weary king was, he could have had no conception of the rate at which books were to be increased later on in the world's history. As we think of it our grief at the burning of two hundred thousand volumes at Alexandria is in some degree assuaged.

For the last fifty years the world has been overwhelmed by the rising tide of a bibliographic flood. It is no longer possible to place boundaries beyond which it cannot pass. Colossal reservoirs like those at Washington have proven ridiculously inadequate. The Oriental metaphor appears on the verge of transformation into a fact: not even the world itself will be able to contain the books that shall be written. The danger that now threatens the race is a new deluge, but of ink. We cannot escape it. We must plunge in, but there is a decided choice among the pools. Some are as clear as crystal; some are the congenial homes of foul mud-monsters. To read anything or everything is as dangerous as to eat anything or everything. The results may be as much more serious as character is of more value than health. As scarcely any other agency has a more marked influence than books upon character, this question of what we shall read is immensely important. Not a few of the dangers to which we are exposed in reading will be avoided by the adoption of some general plan if we keep as well as adopt it. As curiosity is one of the very first and strongest qualities exhibited by most human beings, why not take this as a hint, and begin by reading books that will satisfy our curiosity? Facts are the food which this appetite in a healthy condition craves, and the young person of our day is invited to an absolutely inexhaustible banquet of facts, in spite of Dr. Johnson's assertion—which may have been true when made—that "nothing is so hard to get at as a fact."

What form does your curiosity take? Are you curious to know something about this earth on which you live? about the silent planets above? about your own body and brain? That is natural; that is laudable. And here are books on geology, botany, mineralogy, on astronomy, on physiology and psychology and biology, that will answer just the questions that are, or ought to be, on the ends of your tongues. Are Dana and Gray and Herschel and Hooker and Carpenter and Spencer a little too thorough in their anxiety that none of your questions should be unanswered? Does your mind wander while they are preparing you to understand all the bearings of the answer they are about to make? Then put your questions to men whose intellectual processes are more rapid, if not always so exhaustive.

Just as there is an immense amount of indigestion caused by food not adapted to the tender years of the eater of it, so is there intellectual indigestion and much antipathy caused by an illy-adapted mental diet. You and I might have been very fond of certain sciences from which now we recoil if we had not taken too much of them or in a form too condensed. Our children ought to escape such dyspeptic attacks. All kinds of brain-food, even scientific, are now served in such forms as to be perfectly digestible for the young. There are so-called primers, written with great care and by men of great learning, on each of the sciences, in which you will find your questions answered most simply and interestingly. You will not have the right to set yourself up as an authority on the particular subject about which you have just read a "Primer," but you ought at least to be able to comprehend the force and drift of the arguments used by professed authorities, and you will not feel yourself compelled to give an unqualified assent to the wildest scientific vagaries because you are aware of the fact that you do not know enough to do anything else. The primer will at least have taught you that you must have scientific proof before a theory can be accepted as a scientific fact.

Are you curious to know what has happened to the race of which you are a part since it first found itself on the earth, under the stars? Here stand historians in a long line, from Herodotus to the man who passed you on the street yesterday, all eager and anxious to tell you just what you wish to know. It may help you to choose amongst all these applicants for the office of historical instructor to your High Mightiness to remember what Professor Porter, ex-president of Yale University, says of historians and the two stages to one or the other of which all histories, past, present or future, belong. The first stage, he says, is that of simple narration, though the things narrated may not by any means be simple facts—will probably be in the proportion of one fact to two or more legends. In this stage belong the *Iliad* and the *Odyssey* of Homer and all the mythical stories that have come down to us of heroes like Romulus and Remus and demigods like Theseus and Hercules. To the second stage, in which two marked phases are distinguished, are placed the histories of Herodotus, Thucydides, Tacitus and Cæsar. Here the proportion of fact and fancy or legend is changed. Now the facts largely preponderate; the legend diminishes, till in the last development of this second phase it disappears altogether. We have come now to the critical and philosophical type, the last and highest of which history is capable. We no longer have incredible legends of heroes or interminable lists of war-galleys and phalanxes, or of battles on sea or land, but the causes of things are ferreted out and explained. The development of a nation now overtops in importance the fate of a beautiful woman or that of an extraordinarily strong man. This epoch began, Professor Porter says, with Niebuhr, and all the best historians since have taken their color from it. Every young person should wish to know something of each of these stages, for we cannot understand any one of them unless we have some knowledge of the others; we cannot understand the present without knowing something of the past. It is history that teaches us, as Lowell says, "why things are and must be so, and not otherwise."

We must make a place here, if anywhere, for the newspaper. It has made a very large place for itself, and is supremely indifferent as to whether it is classified or not. It is the most high-handed of all monopolists. It drives all rivals from the field. It excludes with rare impartiality all other forms of printed matter, from the bulky volume to the magazine; and yet this monster of insatiable maw has its rights. The present is of at least equal interest for us with the past. If we are properly curious to know what happened a thousand years ago, why may we not with equal propriety be interested in knowing what happened yesterday? When you read the telegram in your newspaper that Paris had capitulated to the Prussian king and his German allies, you were put in possession of an historical fact of as great significance as the Homeric announcement of the capture of Troy by Ulysses. When you read of the assassination of Abraham Lincoln, you were getting news quite as momentous as that you had read in your ancient history of the murder of Julius Cæsar. The newspaper has its legitimate field if we could but keep it there, but it becomes the tyrant of modern life when it drives out all rivals, as it is doing so effectually that possibly the majority of masculine readers never read anything else. They take their three newspapers a day as regularly as their three meals, lowering the average only a little by reducing the allowance to one on the first day of the week.

Also young persons ought to be specially curious as to the history of their own country. "Know thyself" was the best thing the Delphic oracle ever said in its inscriptions or its utterances. This wisdom is as applicable to the state as to the individual. It is specially applicable to a republic like our own. If we are to have a successful government of the people, for the people, by the people, we the people must know what we are trying to do, and why. It is by no means difficult to find young persons of both sexes who are more familiar with the history of Rome and France and England than with the story of our own nation. That the theme is a vast and intensely interesting one is being recognized by the best historical writers on both sides of the sea. We have no excuse for ignorance when such brilliant and fascinating teachers as the American McMaster and the English Bryce are perpetually ready to enlighten us.

But when your questions—scientific, historical, æsthetic—have been answered and your curiosity has been satisfied, you cannot give over reading if you wish your curiosity to end in culture. Matthew Arnold defines the cultured person as the one " who knows the best that has been thought and said in the world," but one of our own poets lets us look upon a man who knew all these things and had failed of culture:

> "'Twould be endless to tell you the things that he knew—
> All separate facts undeniably true,
> But with him or each other they'd nothing to do.
> No power of combining, arranging, discerning,
> Digesting the masses he learned into learning."

So Burke thought that the cultured man is one who not only is in possession of the facts, but has also " the power of diversifying the matter infinitely in his own mind and applying it to every occasion that arises." It is this power that the study of philosophy should develop. Such reading is not seductively attractive to young people at first. Philosophy, they say, for some one has told them so, is a great circle around which you may make your weary journey only to return to the point from which you started; but in swinging round the circle many interesting, beautiful and useful things may be discovered. About the best way to find out how large a circle is and what's inside of it is to make the circumference of it. Philosophical reading will be of immense advantage to young people if it teaches them the limits of the human mind, the boundaries of thought. Swinging round the circle may save them many a tiresome and dangerous jaunt in quest of panaceas that philosophy, rightly understood, would convince them can have no existence.

Imagination is another faculty of the mind that is hungry for food and that has a right to be fed. There is no dearth of such pabulum. Public libraries, book-stores, news-stands, have their shelves and counters filled with imaginative works. The book you were reading last night—I hope not this afternoon—was a novel. Nine out of ten of the books you will take away with you on your summer vacation will be novels. Four paper-covered novels a day is the allowance that a certain Western lady at one time permitted herself. This is to turn a human being into a gargoyle. Such a stream flowing through the brain can leave behind it nothing but a muddy sediment. Better not read at all than read in such a way. But there are works of the imagination against which no such charge can be laid. Scott and Cooper and Mrs. Stowe and Mrs. Whitney and Charles Dickens and Charles Reade have written novels that have become the fountain-heads of great reforms. The battle of faith and unbelief, Mr. Gladstone and Dr. McCosh think, is to be fought largely for the next fifty years in the pages of romance. Let the book you read be clean through and through. Let it be one that will give you a serious and sensible view of life. Let it be one of high literary merit; and if it be made to take its place among the luxuries, and not the necessaries, such a romance, if it be read not on the sly, but with your parents' consent, may be for you what Spenser calls one of

"The world's sweet inns from care and wearisome turmoil."

All poetical works, from Dante to Shakespeare, from Milton to Whittier, must be classified as works of the imagination. They are not in the strict sense historic, scientific or philosophical, but they may be none the less valuable for that. There are practical, hard-headed—perhaps hard-hearted—men who enter their protest against anything, be it rhythm or blank verse, every line of which begins with a capital. If a man has a thought, why not express it in the sort of language in which we all think? Why dress it up in this fantastic guise? Ah, my hard-headed, hard-hearted friend, poets are born, not made; neither can they be unmade by a protest. Have you forgotten that the Psalms are poems, and that the book of Job is what Carlyle calls the grandest poem ever written?—though, unfortunately, the poetic form is concealed in King James's version in both instances. The Most High has set his approval on poetry, as he did also on imaginative prose, when the Christ spake only in parables. There are many things that it is well for you to deny yourself, but Tennyson, Longfellow, Whittier and Browning do not belong to that category.

If we make a wise use of historical, scientific, philosophical and imaginative books, then material enough will have been gathered for a rich and well-rounded life if all is concentrated upon some worthy purpose. This opens up a field for all inspirational works of every sort. There are numberless books suited to every taste that designedly attempt to imbue their readers with lofty ideals of life. Perhaps the most famous of these are *The Imitation of Christ*, by Thomas à Kempis, and *The Pilgrim's Progress*, by John Bunyan—a book that Macaulay ranks with Milton's *Paradise Lost*.

The biographies of all heroic human souls, of every faith and time, are, though it may be undesignedly, intensely inspirational. From the life of St. Augustine to that of Stephen Grellet and Edward Payson, there is no story of triumph over the unholy trinity of the world, the flesh and the devil that will not ennoble our conception of humanity and fill us with a desire to emulate these godly examples. A well-written biography will be for the unspoiled reader as interesting as a novel, and the substitution of the story of real life for the romance will be an unmistakable gain.

France has just passed through an unexampled literary excitement. A book was thrown almost unheralded upon the market, and was bought up with such avidity that the presses could not supply the demand. It was reviewed at length by the leading newspapers of Paris and the provincial cities. There was but one opinion as to its interest and extreme value. It was not written by any of the popular literary favorites of the day. It was a translation of an old Greek book known to us as "The New Testament of our Lord and Saviour Jesus Christ." Most Frenchmen knew in a vague way that there was such a book. They had heard their priests refer to it and they had seen selections from it in their prayer-book, but very few of them had ever seen a complete copy in French. When Lassarre's translation, with the benediction of the fisherman His Holiness the pope, appeared, it was like a new revelation from Heaven. It was read in the cafés, it was discussed on the boulevards, and it might have been the forerunner of such days as preceded St. Bartholomew's had not the Jesuits become alarmed and persuaded the pope to revoke his benediction, and to place the book on the *Index Expurgatorius*. We have that book in our homes; no papal fulmination can touch it. How often do we read it? Do we permit it to be pushed aside by histories and newspapers and magazines, by works on science and art, by romances and poems, by books of ethics and biography? We make a mistake. This book combines, as no other does, as all others fused into one would not, history, philosophy, biography, high ideals and imperial purposes. "It is the best book that ever was or ever will be written," said Charles Dickens in a letter to his son. "Wherewithal shall a young man cleanse his way? by taking heed thereto according to thy word." Other books may lead you right for a time, and then, from ignorance of the way themselves, leave you in the pathless desert or the trackless forest; but no human being has ever honestly followed this guide that was not brought safe home at last. Better for any of us to neglect reading of any other sort rather than neglect this. We might thus cheat ourselves now and then of some "sweet inn from care and wearisome turmoil;" but if there must be any choice, better cheat yourself of an inn or two along the way than of the eternal home at the end of the journey. Take down from the shelf, where it fell unnoticed months ago behind histories and novels, the Bible your mother gave you, and read with care and attention never before given to it the biography you will find in Matthew, Mark, Luke and John. Read in the book of the Acts and in the Epistles how men's lives were changed by the touch of that life. See how the enthralled of passion and appetite were freed, how the hopeless gained courage, how the restless and objectless found peace and a motive, and as you read the stolid, despairing look in your eyes will fade away. A new hope will steal like a blessed spirit into your heart, and you will dare to do battle with yourself and the world in the inspiration that has come to you from that most human, most divine life.

V.
THE FORMING OF HABITS.

V.

THE FORMING OF HABITS.

"Be not overcome of evil, but overcome evil with good."—Rom. xii. 21.

ARISTOTLE, who was familiarly called "the Surgeon" from the keenness of his intellectual discrimination, was accustomed to say, "A man has formed a good habit when it causes no self-denial." Any act, good or bad, has become habitual when it is performed automatically and involuntarily. The momentum of many choices in the past makes any immediate action of the will unnecessary. It is a condition that has close analogies to slavery where choice and action have no relation whatever. It is not unusual to hear a man confess that "he is a slave to habit."

The grip that habit has upon all human beings results necessarily from our make-up. If we were pure intelligences, with no material enswathment, the power of habit would be lessened, perhaps, to an altogether inappreciable point; but the spirit has its setting in matter: we are resultants of the intermingling of these two diverse elements, and we become, in spite of every effort to the contrary, bundles of habits.

The soul is a prisoner in its invisible holy of holies, and can send out or receive communications only by impressions made on the walls of its dungeon. Light and sound come to it through little apertures easily closed, shutting the captive in to perpetual darkness and silence. Other sensations are carried along prepared channels from the external world to the royal prisoner within. Here is a practically inexhaustible field for the development of habits. The body is not a perfectly flexible instrument for the soul: it permits the soul to express itself only within well-defined limits, and the soul, becoming accustomed to these, ends by accepting the situation. What that situation is to be which is finally accepted depends very largely upon the moral, intellectual and physical habits that are formed before the gristle has altogether turned to bone.

This is the purpose that all wise parents and teachers have before them constantly in dealing with their children and scholars. They try to bring every influence and motive to bear upon both mind and body, that right thinking and right acting may become habitual. Until a child can walk without any conscious effort at balancing itself it does not know how to walk; until it can eat without having to think where its mouth is and how to put the spoon into it, it does not know how to eat; until it can read and write without having to spell each word that is now on the paper or that it wishes to put there, it knows how neither to read nor to write. When the child or the youth or the man does what he has to do without even thinking that he is doing it till his attention is called to it, then he knows that particular thing; it takes its place among the number of his habits.

In the beginning each one of these new automatic actions was difficult, distasteful; there was a disinclination to attempt it which had to be overcome by some reward. There is a celebrated French picture of a great room in the royal palace where the young heir to the throne is being taught to walk. The little fellow is encircled by a crowd of courtiers encouraging him to make the attempt in spite of the risk, but the arguments that are most influential on the royal heart are the ribbons and decorations that the officers take from their own breasts and hold out toward the prince. Then he walks. So you took your first steps because you wanted something—your father's watch or your grandfather's cane. You began to read and write for hope of a sugar-plum or for fear of a whip. But, whatever was the original cause of the action, it left its mark on brain and muscle. It opened up ducts and channels that did not exist before, and along these very soon currents flowed so silently and smoothly that you were scarcely conscious of them.

An old soldier crossing the parade-ground one

day, carrying in both hands a large bowl of soup for his dinner, suddenly heard the ringing command, "Attention!" and, instantly dropping his dinner, he stood erect with hands by his side, while his friends who had played this practical joke upon him chuckled delightedly over the success of it. Long years ago the soldier had been so thoroughly drilled in obedience to that command that when the ear heard the word the order went so swiftly along the well-worn track to the muscle and nerve that there was no time for the judgment to give any opinion whatever in the matter.

It is perfectly true of all mankind, as Paley says, that "they act more from habit than reflection." You became very angry in a moment yesterday. It was wholly unexpected. You were as intent as the old soldier upon something you were doing, when some evil spirit shouted its command, "Fire!" and you dropped everything to discharge an almost fatal load straight at the heart—perhaps of your best friend. You were possibly not very much more to blame for that particular act than the old soldier was for dropping his dinner, but you were to blame for forming the habit of obedience to such evil passions. You were profane yesterday, to your own disgust and that of your friends. You had no expectation of swearing—you had determined that you would not—but the evil spirit uttered its harsh command, and oaths flew from your mouth like stones from a catapult. You told a lie yesterday—the first for many days, and the one just before it was to have been your last. It was not premeditated: you were entrapped into it as the old soldier was into his mistake. Some evil spirit too often obeyed aforetime gave the command, and you did what a moment afterward you were angry at yourself for having done. You made a dishonest bargain yesterday, and the money burns now in your purse. You thought you never would do it again; it seemed to you that there was not money enough in the United States to tempt you to get any of it wrongfully. But there was, alas! It was only a few dollars that you got, but the old enemy and master told you to take them, and it was done before you had time to think. The old soldier only lost his dinner by his involuntary act, but you have lost the respect of your fellow-men and your self-respect and the bright hope you had a little while ago that you were to be henceforth a free man.

We have all formed the habit of giving attention to voices that should be unheard. One would need to speak to an audience of infants in arms who should wish to address those who had formed no bad habits, and even then it would be too late. We may take it for granted, as the apostle does, that the question is not so much of the forming as of the changing of habits. Paul is very outspoken to his friends in Rome concerning some of the bad ways into which they have fallen, but he doesn't consider their condition hopeless. These bad habits, he says, may be overcome by good ones. He has very little faith in any efforts they may make simply to give up doing wrong and break away from old bad habits, but he has great faith in a determination, with trust in God, to do right, and in the forming of new good habits. It doesn't do much good to tear up weeds and leave the ground fallow: it must be sown with grass or grain, and this will fight the weeds and run them out. Tear up your degrading habits, says the apostle, and sow the empty heart with the good seed. You will cease to obey the devil's "Attention!" when you accustom yourself to obey God's "Be not overcome of evil, but overcome evil with good."

Is it possible? Was Aristotle right or was he dreaming when he thought that a good habit may become such a second nature as to cause no self-denial? We may move firmly here, for the solid ground of experience is still under our feet. You have formed some good habits; you are as sure of these as of your bad habits. It is easier for you to do right in some directions than it is to do wrong. You could say the multiplication table correctly in half the time you could give false results to five times six or seven times nine. You speak fairly good grammar with greater ease than you speak bad grammar. You would have to think to make a mistake, and you do not have to think to make a correct sentence. It makes itself; habit does it. It is easier for you ordinarily to tell the truth than it is to do anything else. The channels in your brain are straight, and not spiral. You have got in the habit of seeing things as they are, and of reporting correctly what you see. The shuttles of your brain have become accustomed to weaving a fabric of that particular kind; it would need a change almost as organic as that of putting in new machinery for it to weave lies instead of truths. A musician like Von Bulow or Rubinstein or Hoffman sits at the piano when the twilight has so deepened that your eyes cannot distinguish the black keys from the white, and for hours he dreams in melodies, and his fingers find in the dark all the strange combinations of notes needed to make these dreams audible to your ear. It is all very marvelous, and perfectly natural. Give the musician a pencil and ask him to sketch, or a chisel and ask him to carve, and his movements are awkward and the results ludicrous. New machinery must be created for the new work. It is impossible in a day or a week to make the shuttles that wove harmony, weave outlines and forms. We hear of orators like Burke and Webster and Bright—for whom the English-speaking world still weeps—needing only a great occasion to throw the shuttle, when a magnificent oration was woven with as little effort, apparently, as that with which a loom weaves a carpet, and we are amazed. We forget the years it took to construct the machinery for that particular work; we forget that all the energies of their lives were concentrated upon the production of just those results, and that, therefore, when the hour struck, they had only to release their pent-up energies and the currents were bound to flow along the prepared channels. It was genius back of it all, but it was the oratorical habit that made the production of such orations possible.

And when we hear of men, or see them, that cannot or will not lie, of men who would not by a sign seem to yield assent to an untruth, who found it easier and preferable for them to be thrown to the lions, or to be smeared with oil and bound to a stake in Nero's garden for a living torch, or to have their mouths filled with powder ready to be touched at a signal with a flaming spark, we know that these are men who have persistently cut such grooves in brain and heart and muscle that for them to do anything else than to die for the truth would be most difficult and unnatural. It has so long been their habit to speak the true thing and to do the right thing, irrespective of consequences, that you need not expect them to do anything else because an emperor or a pope or a party commands or entreats something different.

Every choice results in a discharge of energy, and every such discharge breaks channels or deepens those already broken in brain and heart and muscle. So the best physiologists and psychologists are coming to speak as seriously of the momentous importance of little things—of insignificant trifles, as we are tempted to call them—as did the Puritan theologians themselves. It is scientifically certain, they say, that repeated action of any sort tends to make channels out of which it is as difficult for the vital stream to lift itself as for a river to forsake its well-worn bed. Whichever way we turn—toward the evil or the good—we see that Aristotle was right. A man has formed a good habit when it causes no self-denial, and the wise man will enrich his life with such habits; and when others have already been formed, he will replace them, by a process similar to that which created them, by habits of the right sort. He will follow Paul's advice to the very letter: he will fight fire with fire, the evil with good. He will no longer serve the devil because now he serves God.

There are four habits whose desirability is so self-evident that they may be very heartily commended to all young people especially—the habits of industry, church-attendance, Bible-reading and prayer. Paul condenses them all in his rapid sentence: "Diligent in business, fervent in spirit, serving the Lord." The love of work for its own sake is among the rarest of all affections. It may be doubted whether it is ever innate. It is so delightful to enjoy one's self that it needs in almost every instance some pressure from the outside to give us a more serious view of life; yet in a world like this it is impossible for us to do anything of real value for ourselves or others till in some way we have gotten rid of this distaste for work. We are most of us, very probably, hard workers; but if it be from necessity, and not from choice, we are not industrious: we are only obedient to the lash. The moment it ceases to snap we drop into a seat with folded hands and a sigh of relief. Reconstruct your ideas on this subject; do some honest thinking about it. See if it is possible for you to imagine God sending a being so richly endowed as every human creature is into a world where so much needs to be done with the intention that such an individuality should spend a whole lifetime here in doing nothing. Once believe that God wants you to be industrious, and you will have a motive for beginning to work, and for keeping at it till it will become a second nature and no longer cause you self-denial.

As for church-attendance, you do go once in a while when you hear of anything specially attractive or when you feel particularly like it, or even when you don't, if you have some one to go with. You are what has been called "a regular but not indefatigable church-attendant." There are many such to keep you from feeling either shame or loneliness, and possibly to keep you from estimating the habit of church-attendance at its true value. A man may, it is true, go to church regularly all his life and not be much of a man after all, as a man may eat three meals regularly every day and still be but an indifferent specimen of physical development; but in neither case can you lay the blame upon the thing the man does. Had he digested his food as other men do, had he taken the nourishment from the church that other men have done, the results would have been different. Reconstruct your ideas on this subject also. See if it is possible for you to imagine God instituting his Church, commanding his people to become members of it and not to neglect the assembling of themselves together to offer him worship, and to receive instructions from him through his servants, without believing that here is a God-ordained duty, where you have been accustomed to see a man-created privilege of which you did not frequently care to avail yourself. Believe, as you will if you study the question honestly, that God wants you to be a member in, and a regular attendant of, his Church, and you will have a motive for beginning such attendance, and for continuing it till it too will become a second nature and no longer cause you self-denial.

You have read the Bible through—or, at least, the New Testament. It is a book you would heartily commend. You would be glad to lend your copy to a friend at any time without hurrying him to return it. You know a good many biblical conundrums and something in a general way of the book as a whole. But you do not read it anything like as regularly as you read your newspaper or your novel. Your superficial familiarity with it deludes you into thinking you know it well enough now. If a new Epistle should be discovered written by Paul or James or Peter, you would read it at once. So you are half unconsciously placing the book which you really believe to be the word of God on a level with the other books that lie on your table, which are read once or twice and then opened no more. The purpose of reading a revelation from God, we can see at a glance, must be different. Here are our sailing-orders, the chart by which we are to steer, directions complete and minute for our conduct by the way. It is impossible for us to be too familiar with all this. If we knew it by heart, it would be of unspeakable advantage to us. That we ought to consult it as habitually as the ship's captain does the sun, and for the same reason, is indisputable. Select your own time—morning and evening will probably be best—and read this book as regularly as the sun rises and sets. It will not be long before the habit will be formed, and to act in accordance with it will cause you no self-denial.

Prayer is a much more universal act than the reading of the Bible. Men pray to God who have never even heard of his revealed word; men pray to him who can't read it, and who will not read it. They pray as children cry in the night. They are in fear or pain, and the call for help will at least do no harm. You have all prayed many times; but if you should pray many times more in the same way, still it could not be said of you—perhaps you would not wish that it should—that you had the habit of prayer. Neither would it be quite true to say that they are in the habit of praying who are merely in the habit of saying their prayers. Great criminals have confessed that in a long life of open lawlessness they had never neglected once or twice a day to count their beads and mutter a Paternoster, or to kneel and say their prayers in the Protestant manner, but that in all this simulation of prayer there was any real yearning for God and godliness it is impossible to believe. The habit we wish to form is not that of saying certain words at a certain time in a certain position, but it is the habit of expressing gratitude to God for the things he gives us, and of asking for other things we think we need; it is the habit of going to God confidently as in childhood you went to your father or to some wise friend. Such a habit is a greater protection than are hosts of good resolutions or watchful friends. Such a habit will do more to ensure a triumphant life than any other it is possible to mention.

Be not overcome of evil. We shall be if we go out jauntily or carelessly to meet it, or if we go conceitedly and contemptuously, as Braddock went to fight the Indians. We must go sobered by the certainty of danger and of defeat if we are off our guard or do not make the best use of the material we have at hand. We must go believing that there is but one way of overcoming evil, and determined to use that way so persistently that the recognition of any bad habit we may consciously or unconsciously have formed shall be the signal for concentrated effort to replace it with one that is good.

VI.
PERPETUAL YOUTH.

VI.

PERPETUAL YOUTH.

"And entering into the sepulchre they saw a young man sitting on the right side clothed in a long white garment."—MARK xvi. 5.

THE fountain of perpetual youth, for the Christian, is the grave. They who have followed Christ on this side, are to be on the other as the angels of heaven, and this angelic form that startled the women who hurried to the sepulchre was straight and lithe and young, in the "bloom of a life that knows no decay." This "young man," as Mark calls the divine messenger, may have been one of those the patriarch Jacob saw as he slept on his pillow of stone at Bethel and beheld the ladder that reached from earth to heaven, thronged with angels. He may have been one of the two that grasped Lot by the hand as he lingered in Sodom and entreated him to flee to the mountain lest he should be consumed, or he may have been a mortal, tempted and tried like ourselves, but who, conquering at last, as we may, was clothed in white, as all who overcome shall be. An old man perhaps he was when he plunged into the river of death, but in that strange bath his youth was renewed.

We draw back from old age as from the grave itself. They seem to be removed from each other but by a single step. We dread the undignified exposure of human weakness from which but few of the aged can hope to escape with almost the same intensity with which we recoil from the pitiless revelations of the grave, but to be unclothed by age and death is for the Christian to be clothed upon with garments of white and with perpetual youth. The youth we have here is only a poor imitation of that we may have there. It is like a snow statue after one of Michael Angelo's designs. The slightest touch seems to take something from it. You turn your head away for a moment and look back, and you can see the ravages that time has already made upon it. What is so transitory, so evanescent, so illusive, as youth? As long as it is yours you are unconscious of it; and when you begin to congratulate yourself on its possession, already your friends are saying, "How old you look!" and that was your thought about them, though they were born a year or so later than you. The younger children in the home are always pushing the older ones on into society or business, as one season jostles another forward. Each class in school or in college is eager to thrust the one above it into the university or into the world. Youth is gone almost ere one can say it lightens. "I once was young," says David; and we must be very quick indeed if we would not be obliged to put all we say about our youth in the past tense.

But in that land from which the young man who sat in the sepulchre came we are to be given, so he seems silently to assure us, by Him who has conquered death for himself and his own, an æon of years to be young in. We are to feel through long unending centuries an exulting sense of bodily strength. We have just enough of it here to know what it means. For a few hours each day we may sniff the battle afar off, with eager desire to be in the hottest part of it, and then this imperfect instrument of our wills must be reinvigorated and repaired by food and sleep. As walking is simply a perpetual falling and catching of one's self before the act is quite completed, so life, even of the youngest and strongest, is a constant wearing out and renewal in the repair-shops of the dining-room and the sleeping-chamber, till more radical measures are required and the doctor is called in. What a poor imitation all this is of the youth that awaits us just beyond the grave! "They shall hunger no more, neither thirst any more." There will be no necessity to repair with food the wasted strength of that body. "There is no night there." They have no need of long hours for rest and restoration. This body sown in weakness is to be raised in power. The energy in it is to be so full and abounding that renewal would be as superfluous as the renewal of the life that has gone pulsing through the universe with undiminished vigor from the beginning until now. The bloom of its life is to know no decay.

This perfect body is to find itself, as these imperfect bodies of ours never have found themselves in this unharmonic world, in a perfect environment. There will be absolutely no friction. And why should not one be perpetually young in such circumstances? The tasks appointed for this perfect instrument will be wholly congenial. Have you ever found them altogether so here? Has there not always been some undesirable element in quantity or in quality. The work you thought exactly what you wanted, proved to be something quite different, after you had undertaken it. You deceived yourself for a little while by enforced self-congratulation that this was exactly what you wished for, but at last you were compelled to move over to safer and solider ground, and to acknowledge that it was a duty to be performed in spite of certain irremediable unpleasantnesses. It is not the work itself that wears us out and ages us, but the unadaptedness of it, the heat and irritation gendered by it. Why should not they who have nothing to do but to carry out a will with which their own is in perfect harmony keep their youth unbroken? There is no inward recoil from the tasks assigned them, and there is no outward opposition. Whatever retards and sets itself up as a stumbling-block in the onward march of truth and righteousness has been left on this side the river. There are no difficulties there to be overcome, no obstacles to be surmounted, no seductions to be resisted, no assaults to be repelled. How could one grow old in such surroundings?

Theirs is the freshness of an enduring youth; the sparkle of the wine abides. Many a time have we stood

> "Like stout Cortez when with eagle eyes
>   He stared at the Pacific, and all his men
> Look'd at each other with a wild surmise,
>   Silent, upon a peak in Darien;"

but when we descended into the plains beneath and sought the gold whose glistening ingots we were sure we saw from the heights above, we found that the light had been flung back from rocks of quartz and shales of mica. The forests that from the hill-tops looked like Elysian groves in whose cool glades one might walk unwearied for ever, proved to be, as we tried to enter them, dank jungles, impenetrable morasses. Wild beasts were there, and serpents, and fevers more deadly still. It is a land of illusions, this earth on which we dwell, and every year takes many of them from us, and with them goes the sparkle and zest of life. The time is very short in which any mortal, however favorably placed, can be embarrassed by the wealth of pleasures that offer themselves. A few years are quite sufficient to try them all, and the larger part of life remains to be wasted in vain advertising for some new gratification. Why should not they be perpetually young who are constantly finding every cup which they lift to their lips far sweeter than their anticipations? How can they grow old whose ever-renewed experiences compel them to say, "Satisfied! satisfied!" even more often than our experiences here compel us to say, "Vanity of vanities"? "The oldest angels," some one says, "are the youngest." Why not? They are the ones who have been most often satisfied. They are the ones who can begin each new task with greatest zest, and they have had the largest experience of the restful delights of the service on which they are entering.

Theirs is the trustfulness of youth. It is quickly lost here. It withers under the cold winds that sweep across this earth as flowers wither touched by frost. There are vast moral distances between the child that believes in everybody and the man who believes in nobody, but in time the distance may be small that lies between. Confidence is an exotic; we find here but little congenial soil for it. The ground is littered too deep with insincerities and infidelities and hypocrisies for any such growth to take root of itself. In the home it is indigenous, in the school it is thrifty and strong, but in the market-place and the forum it droops, and if not nurtured with greatest care speedily dies. This world offers an abundance of splendid soil for cynicism, for misanthropy, for misogamy. Such seed will take root almost anywhere and grow like a gourd in the tropics. We have each of us a thriving little crop of our own of these things. It is a crop easily sown and raised, but the reaping of it is a sad enough occupation—so sad that before it is half gathered many a man has given up altogether in despair. Woe to you if you are sowing such a crop for yourself, if you are so false to yourself that you cannot believe in the truth of any one else! Woe to you if you are sowing such a crop for others, if through your deceit and insincerity they who once believed are coming to doubt! Woe to you if you are taking from any human soul the faith it once had in purity and truth, in virtue and goodness, in man and God! It must needs be that offences come, but woe to him by whom the offence cometh!

Though the lost faith of your childhood may have returned to you enriched and deepened since you began to believe in Jesus Christ, though you have learned to know him and are perfectly confident that no word of his can ever be too implicitly trusted, yet you are on your guard still against your fellow-men. That form of the child's faith has gone from you irrevocably. It was frittered away by petty little deceits, or it was swept away by some great cruel treachery. You can never again trust your fellow-men as you once did. Not, it is true, in a world where even apostles could betray and deny their Lord, but that trust shall come back to you in that land from which the young man of the sepulchre came. Confidence is in the air there as doubt is in the air here. All souls, as well as all garments, there are white. The language of heaven is not a medium for the concealment of thought, like the language of earth. It may be that there is no language there—that thoughts are seen by the pure eyes of the pure in heart. One glance into souls as clear as crystal will be all that faith will ask to leap at once into vigorous life. Why should not they have perpetual youth whose souls are clean, and who see everywhere only clean souls around them?

These children in the Father's house trust one another with open eyes now as once in early childhood upon the earth they trusted one another blindly. They trust the Father, too, with the old-time confidence of their earliest days in earthly parents, but now it is an enlightened and a reasonable confidence. It was well enough for us all as children to believe that our fathers knew everything and could do everything. Any other feeling about them would have been unnatural. It was a memorable day of great unhappiness when this faith was shaken and we began to have doubts, ending at last in the certainty that there were many things they did not know and could not do. To be in a home again with that old trust back in the heart, and having a right to stay there for ever, would be almost enough in itself to make us feel young once more.

They trust him to tell them all they need to know. There is no hurry. Eternity is around them. The tree of knowledge is above them; its fruit, luscious and ripe, falls into their opened hands. They are coming to know as they are known. Mysteries are being explained in the clear, strong light, as the weird shapes of the night take on familiar forms when the sun rises above the hills. Cycle upon cycle may pass and some questions may still be unanswered, but they are not impatient as we are in this "troublous land of time and dreams." They are entranced by the ever-changing panorama of resolved perplexities that passes before them. Why should not they grow young who are coming to understand all mysteries?

They trust Him to give them all they ought to have. Stars differ from one another in glory. Some who have been last here are first there, but they see the reason for it, as we cannot for the lifting up of one and the casting down of another here. We are never quite satisfied with what comes to us on this side of the grave. If it is not what we asked for, we wonder why; and if it is what we asked for, we wonder that we had not asked for more. Not even the man who said he had learned in whatsoever state he was, therewith to be content, had everything he wanted. He wished to be free from pain, and the thorn yet hung in his flesh. He wished to be free from Roman fetters and prisons, and he was thrust down into a dark dungeon under the pavement. But there contentment is swallowed up in satisfaction. "More than they could ask or think" is flowing in upon them along every channel. The hunger and the thirst of the entire nature is disappearing for ever. Why should not they be young who are harassed by no wants?

They trust him to make them all they wish to be. From the first entering upon that land all ambition to be chiefest vanished they knew not how. They found some such prayer upon their lips as that of an humble saint who cries, as he looks toward that day,

> "I have but thee, O Father! Let thy Spirit
>   Be with me, then, to comfort and uphold.
> No gate of pearl, no branch of palm, I merit,
>   Nor street of shining gold.
>
> "Some humble door among thy many mansions,
>   Some sheltering shade where sin and striving cease,
> And flows for ever, through heaven's green expansions,
>   The river of thy peace.
>
> "There, from the music round about me stealing,
>   I fain would learn the new and holy song,
> And find, at last, beneath thy trees of healing,
>   That life for which I long."

They have begun to see now, as they could not, as we cannot, here, how creatures who have been so unlike their own ideals can be transformed into his perfect likeness. As they feel the work moving on in them they are satisfied to stand still and see the salvation of their Lord. Why should not they be young who have already looked upon that which they are to be?

Theirs, too, is the joyfulness of youth—not the

unthinking and baseless joy of the very young who are light-hearted because they are light-headed, who laugh and sing because they are ignorant of the dangers around them, and whose gladness might be driven away by a single sober, sensible thought; but theirs is the joy of those who have seen danger and have faced it down, who have met enemies and have conquered them. It is the joy of those who have fought the good fight and have finished their course and have kept the faith and have received the crown. Their work is done. All that element of uncertainty that kept them restlessly alert here has for ever been removed. The race is run, and they have won the prize; the battle is ended, and they are victors. Why should youth not flow back into hearts that know such joy as that?

Theirs is the gladness, too, of those who have been permitted to see with Christ the travail of his soul and are satisfied. They have looked, as he has lifted the curtain for them, down through the ages of time that still remain to the end of all things, and as they see the glorious consummation of their Lord's work, as they watch his enemies and those who were eager to sink his name into bottomless oblivion coming eagerly to him with their gifts of gold and frankincense and myrrh, as they behold men of every color and of every tongue bowing before him with every expression of grateful love, kings and philosophers side by side with the most lowly and the most ignorant, how can they help joining in the new and holy song, "Worthy is the Lamb that was slain to receive power, and riches, and wisdom, and strength, and honor, and glory, and blessing"? How can they ever grow old whose hearts are thrilled with the joy of that song?

The oldest person here to-night, looking back, feels that it was but yesterday and he was young, and the youngest person here will be old in a little space of time—as it were, a day. Soon the head will be whitened: "The almond tree shall flourish." The eye will be dimmed: "Those that look out of the windows shall be darkened." The hands shall shake and the feet shall falter: "The keepers of the house shall tremble, and the grasshopper shall be a burden, and desire shall fail." And what then? Must we be dragged on, caught in an endless chain, to weakness, old age and death? Or may we so use our youth as to have within us the assurance that it may become perpetual? Are there not limits, prophecies, of it, that like the angel of the sepulchre give us hope, as we look into their faces, that we shall for ever be young? Are there not potent qualities that even here seem to renew the youth of those who have grown old? At thirty-four, James Watt, the inventor of the steam-engine, was an old man. "I greatly doubt if the silent mansion of the dead is not the happiest place," he wrote. At eighty, two young men found a day spent in his company among the most amusing and instructive, so one of them says, of his whole life. What was it that changed the old-young man into a young-old man? It was not good health or good luck, for his health never was very good and he had his full share of bereavement and disappointment, but it was a new way of looking at life. He had come to see that he might give over living for himself—a way of living that had almost burned up his energies before his days were half finished—and that he might begin to live for God and for the help of humanity. It was that new purpose that gave him back the zest and confidence and joy he had wellnigh lost. Will you live for yourself and be old in body and soul while you are yet young in years? or will you live for God and for the good that you can do, and like James Watt be young in body and in soul long after the first page of the old family Bible has proved in black and white that you are very aged indeed? Will you waste your youth in a giddy round of sensuous pleasures till you drop into a jejune and hopeless old age with no future to look forward to in time or in eternity? or will you use your youth so wisely as to be young still when old age comes, and with such vital germs within you that you shall rise out of the grave clothed upon, like the messenger whom the Marys saw at the empty sepulchre on that Easter morning, with white raiment and perpetual youth?

VII.
TEMPTATION.

VII.

TEMPTATION.

"Let no man say when he is tempted, I am tempted of God; for God cannot be tempted with evil, neither tempteth he any man: but every man is tempted, when he is drawn away of his own lust and enticed."—JAMES i. 13, 14.

TEMPTATION proves that we are neither angels nor devils. If we were altogether good or bad, the word would have no meaning for us. We should move straight forward then into the ever-deepening light or darkness, with no allurement to turn aside. That we can be tempted we must consider rather as hopeful than discouraging. We none of us lose any supposed honor by the assurance that we are not perfect, and the discouraged and despairing may gain much by the certainty that they are still capable of an exclusively human experience.

Temptation itself is not more natural to man than the offering of excuses for having yielded to it. It was exceedingly easy for a Greek or a Roman to release himself from all responsibility of an unpopular or shameful act. He had only to say, if caught stealing, "My god Mercury enticed me;" or if discovered intoxicated, "My god Bacchus allured me to drink;" or if found beating out his enemy's life, "My god Mars made me do it;" but a Christian—one of the apostles of Jesus Christ—pricks with his pen this consoling theory of a false theology. "Don't deceive yourself in that way," James says. Don't flatter yourself that a god had any part in the meanness of which you are accused. The only god there is in this universe is good. "Let no man say"—be he Greek, Roman or Hebrew—"when he is tempted, I am tempted of God, for God cannot be tempted with evil, neither tempteth he any man: but every man is tempted, when he is drawn away of his own lust and enticed."

When you do wrong, there is one person to blame for it, and that is the one who does the wrong. It is not denied that other people or other things may have been the occasion of it, but these outward enticements, however attractive, would have been impotent had not your consent been given. We say we are tempted by our senses. We try—half unconsciously, perhaps—to make the eye or the ear do duty as scapegoat, as the Greeks once made scapegoats of their gods. But the eye and the ear only carry impressions to the soul, and they are no more to blame for what follows the delivery of their message than is the messenger-boy for what you may do after you read the telegram he hands you. Every man is tempted—not when he is drawn away of his eyes or of his ears, but of his lusts. Two pair of eyes look at the same object; and if you could photograph the impressions made on those four optic nerves, the pictures might be almost identical, but the results upon those two lives were very different. One of these pairs of eyes belonged to a drover just in from the Far West, and the other belonged to his daughter; and the object they saw was a jewel in a shop-window. They both saw it, but the cattleman's heart made no response—he wouldn't give the poorest colt on his farm for it—but that girl there by his side has had some education. She has read about courts and about crown-jewels. She knows that that sparkling thing is a diamond, like those worn by empresses. It is a small one, to be sure, that no empress of good standing would want, but this little lady thinks she never saw anything so beautiful; her heart is in her throat as she looks at it. She is really tempted to break the tenth commandment in a way she could not even explain to her father. They go down the street, and hear on the next corner sounds coming out intermittently as a door swings to and fro—snatches of songs, boisterous laughter and the clicking of glasses. They both hear them. The father stops as if fascinated, but the daughter clutches his hand and tries to drag him by. It was not the jewel that tempted the daughter nor the dram-shop the father: it was something within them that leaped up as traitors will when the signal is given and the time seems to have come to betray the fortress.

This is why it is that, while we all live in the same world and see, many of us, the same things, no two human beings ever have exactly the same temptations. There is nothing in any of our senses, there is nothing in the surroundings of any of us, business, professional, social, that makes sin necessary. When we are drawn away, it is by our own lusts to which we have given assent. That some sights and sounds and places are more dangerous than others is altogether unquestionable. What these are for us is one of the things that we ought all to know about ourselves. Perhaps there is as little common sense used in resisting temptation as in any other phase of human life whatsoever. We learn, for the most part after a few trials, that we are better off physically if we avoid some things and secure others. If we find we can't get along well without eight hours' sleep, we make an effort to sleep eight hours; if we find that there are dainties we cannot eat without resulting discomfort, we refuse them, however delicious they may be to the taste; but we seem to lose our heads when we get on to higher ground where the questions to be decided have to do more directly with our moral than with our physical well-being. The process up to a certain point is the same as that with which we are familiar. There is the effort to assimilate some particularly delicious indulgence, repeated more than once, with a never-failing moral and spiritual discomfort resulting, but there the resemblance ceases.

We do not avoid these things as we do for the most part those that express themselves in physical terms. We are as stupid about it as if we had no moral memories whatever. A man knows that if he exposes himself at certain times and in certain atmospheric conditions his system will be unable to resist, and he knows with the same degree of certainty that if he exposes himself to unfavorable moral and spiritual conditions he will undoubtedly succumb; but he does it, not only once or twice: he keeps on doing it. He deliberately embarks in a business that from the very nature of it reproduces constantly these unfortunate conditions. He associates himself with men in whose society he finds these conditions are never absent. He reads books in every line of which lurks moral malaria. He chooses his home in a place that makes escape doubly difficult, and after he has done everything that one could think of to dig pitfalls for himself he tumbles into them, and says, "I am not to blame. No one could have escaped under these circumstances." Yet these men in their self-constructed pitfalls serve at least one purpose, if no other—that of a warning to the young not to throw overboard common sense when they know that just ahead are the rocks where sirens sit and sing. Let them counsel you as the half-repentant Circe, daughter of the Sun, counseled Ulysses so to prepare his ship by filling the ears of the sailors with wax and having himself bound to the mast that it might not be easy—nay, might be impossible—for them to yield to the seductive song. There are many enchanted islands just ahead. To sail on thoughtlessly till the music of those fascinating songs fills the air will be fatal. Make preparation for such moments. See to it that the ears and the hands are properly cared for.

But Orpheus took even a better way than that of Ulysses. When he passed the same island of the sirens, he left his own hands unbound and the ears of his sailors unstopped, but he made sweeter music on his harp than that of the sirens, and he and all his men could smile at the vain efforts of their would-be destroyers. This is "the expulsive power," as Chalmers calls it, "of a new affection." This is the common-sense and Christian way of resisting temptation. Let your tempted soul hear sweeter music than the sirens make if you would keep contentedly on your course. The majority of those who give themselves over to gross, sensuous lives do it as much because they know of nothing else that would be interesting to do as for any other reason. Could they have become engaged in any form of healthful activity, the power of the temptation over them would have been immeasurably diminished.

The man who is hard at work, especially if it be in the kind of work he likes, will not often hear the song of the sirens; and if he hears it, he will be too absorbed to give his attention to it.

All young men and women ought to be regularly employed. If they do not need to work to keep soul and body together, they do need it to keep the soul clean and the body pure. If you are compelled to labor to earn a living, do not look upon it as a curse: God may have seen that it was the only way to save you from the curse of sin. If you have nothing to do, look for work at once; there is an abundance of it to be found if you do not care for pecuniary remuneration. There is work to be done in getting work for those who cannot live without it. There is work to be done for those who are suffering because they are too old or too young or too weak to work. There is work to be done in visiting the sick and those who are in prison—work in teaching the ignorant and in reforming the vicious, in clothing the naked and feeding the hungry, in giving comfort to the sorrowing and courage to the hopeless. Don't say, "That sort of work is for ministers and priests and sisters of charity." So it is, but not for them exclusively. So far as we know, there was not a single representative of any of these classes in that company to whom Christ said, "I was an hungered, and ye gave me no meat; I was thirsty, and ye gave me no drink; I was a stranger, and ye took me not in; naked, and ye clothed me not; sick and in prison, and ye visited me not."

Learn as well to make a proper use of the pure, ennobling pleasures of life. Let their sweet songs drown the seductive songs of the sirens. Train yourself to admire and enjoy a beautiful sunset or a still more beautiful sunrise. Let the eye be refined in its tastes till a field of ripening grain, a long slope of green grass, a river winding through a valley, a blossoming orchard, a snow-clad mountain, a stretch of blue sea, shall give a keener sense of enjoyment than the garish splendors of halls devoted to sensuous delights. Learn to admire and enjoy the best there is in art. The world's masterpieces for the most part are on the other side of the sea, but these are by no means necessary for the development of the artistic sense. There are galleries of fairly good pictures open to us all here in our own city. An hour spent in one of them would be of more advantage to you than many hours spent in watching the changing scenes, too often contaminating, of the theatre or the opera-house. There is real art now in the illustrations of our best magazines, brought by free libraries within every one's reach. Learn to see and to feel the beauty there is in the simplest scenes well drawn or etched, and you have a source of pleasure that will neither vitiate nor satiate.

Music may be even more helpful than pictures. It is cheaper. There is more variety and greater intensity in the pleasure it gives. If we are at all musical, we can carry our treasures with us everywhere, and can bring them out by night as well as by day for the delectation of our friends and for our own gratification. To be able to play on an instrument, or to use that most noble of all instruments the human voice, is to be possessed of an unfailing source of the purest pleasure. Though there are comparatively few who can ever hope to play or to sing well enough to give gratification to really critical people, yet the world does not exist altogether for the benefit of really critical people; and if you can learn to play or sing or whistle a tune, you will have it in your power at any time to overwhelm the siren's song with safer and nobler melodies, even if they are not very artistically rendered.

Literature offers quite as real a pleasure to even a larger number of people. Most musical amateurs spend more hours a day with their books than with their instruments or songs. Johnson thought the most miserable man in all the world "is he who cannot read on a rainy day." He might have enlarged the rainy day a little and made it include all odd and unoccupied moments. Probably the majority of us have received more pleasure from books than from all other sources combined. Blessed are the young men and maidens who ask no keener delights than those they know are always awaiting them between the covers of a good book. If you do not care now for reading, set yourself as determinedly to acquire this taste as you would if you knew that on the last page of every worthy book you should read you would be certain of finding a legal-tender bill of a large sum, so bewitched by book-loving fairies as not to be plucked by any possibility till every page is read.

The actual rewards to those who read the whole of a good book are greater than any within the power of fairies to distribute. Not the least of these will be the independence you will thus achieve. Instead of being a hanger-on of every friend or acquaintance who can amuse you and save you for an hour or so from yourself, you will be absolutely free to seek society of any sort or to avoid it, as may seem desirable. You know you have better than the best to be found in modern drawing-rooms in your own little library, though there may be only a dozen books upon the shelf. Outranking even this priceless benefit will be the moral and spiritual gains you will have made. At the first notes of the siren's song you can fill the air with the sweetest music of the world's purest and most inspiring poets; you can enchain the ear with the eloquence of the grandest orators that have ever lived; you can entrance the eye with pageants that move across the page more brilliant and splendid than have ever marched across any Field of the Cloth of Gold.

Thrice blessed are the young men and maidens to whom the Bible is the most interesting of books. An audience of colored people can be gathered anywhere in the South, it is said, by an announcement that a number of chapters will be read from either the Old Testament or the New. They delight in the long musical roll of the Psalms, in the wide wondrous visions of the prophets, in the exquisite parables of Christ and in the cogent Epistles of Paul. Many of the greatest scholars here in the North and in England and Germany are of the same mind as the ignorant freedmen. To them, as to Sir Walter, this is "the Book." There is no other comparable to it. They would choose it unhesitatingly if they knew they were about to be cast away upon a lonely island, and could have but one book. A vast amount of intellectual error, often of a painful, and sometimes of a very dangerous, sort is altogether avoidable for those who are willing to be admonished by this book, and there is moral and spiritual life and health in it for the whole race. Blessed are they who when they are tempted are able at once to grasp the sword of the Spirit, which is some word of God, as Christ himself did.

As Christ himself did! It is only in the companionship of this Christ who met the tempter and conquered him for us that we can be absolutely secure against temptation. All the contentment we can find in our work, all the pleasure and inspiration we can get out of nature and art and music and literature, all the moral and spiritual strength that leap from this word as waters leap from a spring, will be of incalculable advantage in lessening the frequency and power of temptation; but when it comes upon us and the storm breaks, then we must fly to this Lover of our souls. Our safety depends very largely in our reliance upon his presence and help, and that reliance will be affected in no small degree by our ability to realize his constant nearness. There is a great difference in temperaments as to this power of seeing the invisible. There are some, like the old Greek philosopher, who can see goodness incarnated, and who are entranced with the form of beauty outlined before them with a distinctness almost like that of a material presence; there are Christians who seem to live in the conscious presence of their Lord as really as did they who journeyed with him across "those sacred fields;" but there are others to whom all this is largely incomprehensible. They believe in Christ as they do in goodness, but they have never seen either. They lose very much, much more perhaps than there is any need of their losing. If they would make a rational use of these four inspired pictures of the Christ, he would no longer be for them a Christ entombed in a garden or a Christ enthroned in heaven: he would be the Christ of his own promise, "with us always even unto the end," and to whom we can cry when we feel ourselves sinking, as Peter did, and there is time only for a cry, with perfect confidence that he will hear and answer our agonizing appeal as quickly as he did Peter's.

The old mythology has passed away altogether. Men long ago ceased to believe in gods, impure themselves and tempting mortals to vice. "God is God: there is none other," is the message that even the

Mohammedan shouts in the ears of Asiatic and African savages. He will not entice to sin; he died to save the world from it. He lives for the same purpose. He does not see fit to remove us altogether from the sphere of temptation, but that need not disquiet us: "he will not suffer us to be tempted above that we are able, but will with the temptation also make a way to escape." Never permit yourself to believe or to be persuaded that temptation, in whatever form it comes, is irresistible. It is for all of us if we stand alone, but for none of us who have "the right man on our side, the man of God's own choosing."

VIII.
MAKING A HOME.

VIII.

MAKING A HOME.

"Through wisdom is an house builded; and by understanding it is established."—Prov. xxiv. 3.

THE idea of the family is one of the ideas that are as widespread as is the human race. Instinct reproduces something like it even among birds and animals, but the home is altogether a human idea and confined to man in his civilized state. There are families in Asia and in Africa, and perhaps in Europe and in America, whose dwelling-places are no more real homes than are the lairs in which wild beasts live. There are sociologists who believe that the home is found only in civilization, and in civilization north of a certain latitude. They make it coterminous with the frost-line: "Where ice never forms, homes are not made." Where the climate is so mild all the year round that every one lives out of doors, coming into the house only to sleep, the idea of the home is a dormitory. In the north, where the nights are long and the winters severe, the family is driven in upon itself, and the home crystallizes within as silently as the ice without.

But it does not follow that every family living

under a weatherproof roof north of the frost-line is in a home. Strangely enough, none of the European peoples, from the far south to the land of almost perpetual snow, use the word "home" at all; it is not in their languages. They get no nearer to it than "house." "To the house," "in the house," are the idioms they use for "going home" and "at home." In English the word is one of the most common and one of the most sacred; it is next to the word "heaven" itself. In this land of homes Philadelphia bears the proud distinction of being the "city of homes." One other city has more families, but has far fewer homes. Communists and socialists grind their teeth at the very mention of Philadelphia; they consider it an almost barren soil for their theories. The material out of which a destructive and murderous mob may be formed does not come from the home. But cities, like men, often end by failing at their supposed strongest point. That—at least, they think—can take care of itself. It is left unguarded, and there the enemy enters. As soon as the making of homes and the fostering of home-life come to be questions in which it is supposed that Philadelphians need take no interest, our glory will at once begin to grow dim. Your parents had to answer for themselves questions concerning home-making, and you cannot adopt their decision: you must make a home for yourself.

"Wisdom," Solomon says, "builds the house," the term in which he would probably include the home-idea as well as that of the family-name, "and understanding solidifies it." Our American Solomons for the most part believe that the sentence should be amended to read, "By money is a house builded, and by money is it established." That money can build timbers and bricks and mortar and stone into something that answers to the term "house" is undebatable. There are almost as many architects as lawyers on Chestnut and Walnut streets, and they will promise for a certain sum to draw a plan and make all contracts with the builders, and have you a house put up and furnished, to the very dishes on the table if you wish, within a limited time. By adding half as much again time and money to their estimates you may be reasonably confident that the promise will be fulfilled. Money will build you a house, it will give you an "establishment," but it cannot assure you a home. The French call these massive structures that money builds "hotels." Perhaps it would not be unfair to press a partial confession out of the word that the life within those walls is not unlike that of a hotel. The inmates may have as few common interests as have the so-called "guests" of one of our great caravansaries. But by diminishing the size you do not necessarily increase the home-feeling. There may be second- and third-class, as well as first-class, hotels. Wherever money is the only reliance, there can be nothing but a hotel or a boarding-house. To have a home there must be unity of feeling, community of interests, and money is notoriously unable to produce either.

If we cannot amend this sentence of Solomon's by replacing the word "wisdom" by "money," might we not, a large number of young people are always asking, replace it by "love"? They go forth hand in hand, these trusting couples, relying on love to lead them to some vine-clad cottage in which they can build a home. Alas that Love, proverbially blind, should lead so many to the poorhouse or the divorce courts! Love was never yet caught handling brooms and dustcloths and frying-pans, or filling the larder with things to eat and the closets with things to wear. While neither cleanliness nor plenty makes a home, it is next to impossible to make a home without both. Love must have at least one part wisdom added to it before it can be effective as a home-maker, and then it becomes so permeated all through with wisdom that it is almost certain to succeed.

Love of that sort has no false pride: it is willing to begin at the bottom. It doesn't care how high society may lift its supercilious eyebrows: it is ready for any honest toil that may offer. It is not frightened at burdens that might appal one brave heart, for in this house there are two brave hearts that can smile at a little load like that. "Those were our happiest days," say some of those home-builders now grown old and rich, "when we began the making of our home. When there was plenty of hard work, with usually enough to eat, what mattered it if now and then we sat down to rather a meagre or an ill-cooked meal?" Wisdom had come a little short in providing and preparing, but it had done its best; and love could afford to overlook any deficiency.

In such a home, where there are wise as well as tender eyes in each head, the importance of other things besides the table will be recognized. There is an indescribable atmosphere that is quite as essential to the home as good bread and enough of it. What some of the qualities are that tend to create this atmosphere, and without which it cannot exist, is an open secret. Courtesy is one of these. Those who have entered into an engagement to make a home together, or who have just begun the work, are ordinarily so courteous to each other as at once to betray themselves. This ought to bring a blush, not to the faces of these young innocents, but to the colorless, wrinkled cheeks of those who smile. It is the most terrible confession of their own deficiency in that quality of which neither the betrothed nor the newly-wedded ever has too much. These old cynics were once themselves as courteous as the young bride and groom that have aroused their merriment, but their courtesy waned with the moon, to wax, alas! no more. The ears that were accustomed to the gentle speech of the bygone halcyon days would not recognize the harsh voice of the present had they not gradually become accustomed to its increasing gruffness of tone. Where is the table across which those who have celebrated their silver, or even their crystal or tin, wedding always speak as they ought? "They are more natural now," do you say? Then to be more natural for most people means to be more brutal. The fine atmosphere of the home cannot be produced by words, however tender, but it can easily be destroyed by rude, uncourteous speech.

Thoughtfulness is another quality as essential as oxygen to the atmosphere of the home. The occupants of a house or a hotel may be courteously indifferent to one another, but in the home this is impossible; such indifference immediately turns what was a home into a house or hotel. The home is the only double-headed entity of which we have any knowledge that is not a monster, but there is no monster comparable to a home in which these two heads are not sympathetic. The duties of the husband and those of the wife are so different that it will require some effort on the part of both to give to each their proper emphasis and importance. It is easy for each to accuse the other of exaggeration, absolute or relative. The wife thinks the husband overparticular about his shop or office or store, and he thinks she underestimates somewhat the obligations of his business or professional life and overestimates the home-claims that bear most directly upon her. Both are very likely right, and both are very likely wrong. There is a mutual failure in thoughtfulness. In love they prefer each other to all the world, but "in honor preferring one another" has quite slipped out of their minds. So with their varied tastes as well as their duties. No two people ever did have exactly the same likes and dislikes, though for a time they may honestly have tried to make themselves and each other think they had. Gradually in every instance where it was not suddenly these differences make themselves felt. The husband and the wife find that æsthetically and intellectually and gastronomically they are not one, but two. If each is self-assertive and confident that the other ought to yield and replace present tastes with the superior appetencies of the other, the fine atmosphere of that home is in danger of losing an essential quality. A little thoughtfulness on the part of each would make it self-evident to both that these differences must exist, that they are essential if the husband and the wife are to be the complement of each other, and that the life of each will not lose in any degree, but will gain markedly, by a thoughtful consideration of these differences.

They have different weaknesses, too, as well as tastes. One is strong just where the other is not, and it seems rather aggravating to both that it should be so. Mistakes that we do not make ourselves appear to us unnecessary and inexcusable. The man forgets that his wife is a woman, and she reciprocates by forgetting that he is a man. He comes home at night from the experiences of a most trying day. Everything has gone wrong.

He couldn't do his own work half as well as usual, and his employés were still more stupid. Some investments turned out badly, or a bill owing him that was marked good proved to be very far from it. His home seems specially attractive in anticipation. He feels the need of it. He opens the door, and the frown on his manly brow deepens. His reception is not what he was counting on. No one meets him. There is no indication that he was expected and that his coming was looked forward to with pleasure. His wife is out, or she is taking care of one of the children or seeing to some domestic duty. When she appears, she seems preoccupied, and looks as if she expected to receive sympathy instead of giving it. She too has had a hard day. The children have been fretful, the servants, if there are any, have been unreasonable, and even the culinary implements have shared the general perverseness of things. She has been looking forward to her husband's return, to the comfort of his presence and the encouragement of his words, but after a single look into his face she too is disappointed. Could they for a little moment exchange eyes, each would get what each craved, each would see that the strength of the other had been somewhat overtaxed, and due allowance would be made; but, for lack of this thoughtfulness, the fine atmosphere of the home is likely to be seriously disturbed, and possibly another proof given the cynical crowd of onlookers that they are right about it, of course, and " marriage is indisputably a failure." It always is when the purpose of it is not the making of a home, but the gratification of a momentary preference exalted by a noble name to which it has no right, or when it is chosen as the surest and easiest way of drawing the envious congratulations of one's friends, or as an escape from *ennui,* or as the last reformatory hope of the worn-out epicurean. Marriage in each of these instances is a predestined failure; but even when the marriage is one of those that appear to have been made in heaven, it will have come short of the perfect ideals that exist in the place where it was made, and even of the somewhat imperfect ideals of the contracting parties. Such a wife and mother as Monica was has pointed out her own failures, which she thought were many. The most perfect home that has ever been formed since Adam and Eve made their great mistake in Paradise has lacked something; but to write the word "failure" over the institution itself on this account would be to condemn as absolutely worthless everything there is this side of heaven.

Every true home must be founded on unselfishness. It does not exist for the husband: that would be the tyranny of strength; or for the wife: that might be the tyranny of sweetness; or for the children: that would be the tyranny of weakness and ignorance; but it exists for all the members of it. "Bear ye one another's burdens" would be peculiarly appropriate as a home motto, though it has failed, apparently, to achieve popularity of that sort.

Such a home, while the most desirable environment for a man or a woman, rises to the point of a necessity for the child. As a place for bringing up children the home has stood, since Plato's unsuccessful experiment, without a rival. "What France needs," said Napoleon as his keen eyes detected the moral and physical degeneration of the people of which he had made himself emperor—"What France needs is mothers." That was only half the truth, as he knew very well. He wanted the fathers to fight his battles and to win new crowns for the collection he was making, or he would have said, "What France needs is homes." There is little hope for France, or for any other country that has that crying need, until it is met in some good degree. American fathers are not prevented by force, as the French were under Napoleon, from doing their best to satisfy that need here, but there are forces almost as potent as the despotic will of Napoleon that hinder and destroy whatever wish of that sort many men may have. Business and politics are as exacting masters as was the ambitious Corsican. They draft men into their exclusive service from extreme youth to extreme old age. They monoplize not only their time, but their thoughts and interests, in a way that Napoleon might have envied. If a man is altogether engrossed with public duties, however honorable in themselves, let him not attempt to build a home: his failure is foredoomed. And let not the man who has begun to build a home think that any other duty, of any sort whatever, can be of greater importance. The men who are compelled to work from early morning till late at night are fortunately very few indeed in this favored country, but the men who use the entire day, evenings included, to further mercantile or professional or political ambitions, alas for their homes! are very numerous. The masculine element is just as essential as the feminine in the household. The fatherhood is as important as the motherhood in the home. We may be ready to question this because so many homes still exist and thrive in a way in which the element of fatherhood is altogether lacking. But if the father had fulfilled his duty, not as well as the average father does, but as well as the average father might, who can tell but that that home might have risen as high if the wing of motherhood instead of fatherhood had been broken? As one of the two, as chief of the two contractors, who have engaged to build a home under your roof, you have no right to give the evenings that should be used in that work to your ledger or your newspaper or your club or your lodge. It will be better for you to be able to say at last "Here am I, Lord, and the children that thou hast given me," than to be able to say, "Here am I, Lord, with a great fortune that I have gathered, or a great name that I have achieved; but, as for my children, their mother will report for them."

For we cannot succeed in separating the two worlds altogether from each other. You may feel sometimes as if there was nothing in your business that could be of any interest to the angels of heaven, but in your home, with your children in your arms, you can easily understand Christ's love for the little ones; and those texts about "their angels always beholding the face of their Father who is in heaven" speak to your heart even though the impression they leave upon the brain is not altogether distinct. How can you help thanking God for your children? How can you turn your back in the morning upon your home without asking him to protect them? You have to be early at the store or office? Yes, but you can always be there a few minutes earlier if it is important enough; then you can take that time for your home. You can use it in reading a few verses from the Bible or in offering a few words of prayer. You haven't the courage to do it? Think what a confession you are making! You wouldn't like to have any one else charge you with such cowardice. Of all places on the earth, your home should be the one where you should be freest to express your truest self, however bunglingly at first, where there is no dread of misapprehension and ridicule. He must be a very small man indeed who in such surroundings dare not hear his own voice repeating the Lord's Prayer or offering some simple sentences of praise or petition. You need the grace that will be given you at such a time as much as your wife needs to know that hers are not the only prayers that rise for your home, and as much as your children need to see the man they think the wisest and best and strongest in the world on his knees before his God. They may have the very best instruction in the Sunday-school and from the pulpit in after-years, but nothing will ever impress them like those earliest memories of the family altar where you, the father, used to pray. Love, courtesy, thoughtfulness, unselfishness, cannot build a home without prayer. "Except the Lord build the house they labor in vain that build it."

Home and heaven! Christ has joined them so closely together that it is hard for us to disassociate them in our thoughts. There is no spot upon earth in which there is so much of heaven as in a true home. Heaven does indeed lie about the infancy of every child born into such surroundings, and the home seems like a perpetual pledge of heaven. "In my Father's house are many homes. I go to prepare one for you." For a few years only, at the longest, can the homes we are building here endure. When some morrow's sun shall rise, its light will fall upon closed shutters, and in the darkness of that house only the ruins of a home will remain; but the love and thoughtfulness and unselfishness and faith that once made a home there are not dead. They are potent still; and when a few more suns shall have risen and set, the home that has disappeared altogether from earth will have been rebuilt for ever in heaven. "Oh, happy home! Oh, happy children there!"

IX.
STRENGTH.

IX.

STRENGTH.

"Finally my brethren, be strong in the Lord and in the power of his might."—EPH. vi. 10.

WE are born with an admiration for physical strength. It is unconscious and instinctive. When the infant prefers the father's arms to the mother's, if it ever does, its cry is an expression of the high value it places upon a firm grasp and a steady step. The pictures the boy cuts from illustrated newspapers and hangs on the walls of his room are those of athletes. So are the portraits, for the most part, that hang in the world's gallery of heroes. There stands old Hercules leaning on his club, with the Nemean lion at his feet. There is great Theseus grappling with the centaur and about to give the hitherto invincible monster his quietus. There is Samson scattering the Philistines right and left with the ridiculous jaw-bone of an ass that becomes terrible in those awful hands. There is David whirling his sling and sending the smooth stone into the white spot between the shaggy brows of the giant, and cutting off that bison-like head with a colossal sword. There to this day on the walls and the propylæa of Egyptian temples is the conqueror Rameses holding his captives by the hair of their heads, while he towers, by the flattering strokes of the sculptor's chisel, many feet above them.

The world will never outgrow its admiration for strong muscles and sinews. The Olympian games are no more, but the popular idol still is the stroke-oar of the successful crew, the pitcher of the champion baseball nine, the bowler of the eleven that holds the cup, the rusher of the football team that wins the ball. The Christianity that equips its young men's associations with model gymnasia and athletic grounds certainly has no word of contempt for physical development. It may, and does, have something to say about moderation in these things, and concerning a tendency, particularly marked in our colleges, to over-estimate the value of brawn as compared with brain. It is not the best scholar, but the best athlete, in his class who is the most envied man of the college. Christianity, common sense and history all make their protest against this as a false appraisement, an untrue perspective—as the judgment of an untrained eye.

The very people that once took the most intense pleasure in physical triumphs began, after a time, to see that this was not the line for man to put himself upon. The brutes were all superior to him here, and in any fair test of strength or speed or endurance man must always come out decidedly second-best. The clearest-eyed of the Greeks saw the mistake, and did what they could to lift man to a higher level, the intellectual, where they felt he belonged, and where the brutes could no longer be his competitors. They succeeded so well that the honors once given to the runner and the thrower and the fighter were very largely transferred to the poet and the orator and the philosopher. The man who could recount in prose or verse the deeds of warriors was sure of a glory that might rival, if not outshine, that of the warriors themselves. Intellectual development was sought as eagerly as physical had been. With the exception of college-students, all men to-day who have sufficient education to give their opinions any value rank intellectual strength above physical. They agree with Bacon "that knowledge is power." They would not for a moment think of comparing the strength of a Samson or a Hercules with that of a Homer or a Humboldt. One, they see, is altogether animal, perishing as utterly after a few years as that of a lion or an elephant, while the other is altogether human and will endure as long as human languages are able to hold human thoughts in solution.

So far we may go with the majority; but if we attempt to rise to a still higher level, we must expect to find the number with us diminishing. Still, there is a very respectable minority who rank strength of will and purpose above both intellectual and physical strength. Not a Hercules nor a Homer is so strong a man, in their eyes, as a Moses or a Washington, enduring reproach or misapprehension without swerving for a single step from the course they had marked out as right. There are political exiles in Siberia, it is said, some of them women of high rank and fine culture, accustomed to the delicate life of the Russian capitals, who have passed long years of unspeakable torture in circumstances that seem to us, as we read, absolutely un-unbearable even for men of the coarsest fibre, who say little in the way of vituperation, but who calmly announce their unalterable conviction that while "they may die in exile, and their children may die in exile, and their children's children may die in exile, at last something will come out of it." Such an exhibition of strength as that thrills every heart that is in the right place as no possible physical or intellectual triumphs could ever do.

This strength of will is so closely allied to moral strength, if they are not one and the same thing from different sides, that it is often exceedingly difficult to distinguish between them. These exiles in Siberia cannot be merely self-willed or obstinate: they must have a firm conviction that they are doing right and to do differently would be a violation of conscience. It needs only to widen the horizon which we presume them to have to include every violation of conscience to give us a glimpse of one of the least common but most exalted types of strength. Shakespeare assumes that strength of this sort is by no means always associated with great physical power when he says,

> "Oh, it is excellent
> To have a giant's strength, but it is tyrannous
> To use it like a giant."

Physical prowess, uncontrolled by justice, right conscience, is utterly denuded of all its beauty in Shakespeare's eyes, and should be in ours. Why should we even account it entitled to the name? Is it not an absurdity to speak of a man as being strong who can be turned this way or that by any wind that blows upon him? Is he strong who has no self-control, who is run away with by temper or by appetite or by desire, who yields with but the show of a struggle to his lust for gold or pleasure or place? Is he a strong man who has not strength enough to do what he believes to be the right thing, though his friend or his party assure him that it will be dangerous to his interests and theirs? Is he a strong man who trembles at the crack of some boss's whip, or who dare not speak because the command, "Keep still!" has been passed along the ranks? The strong man must be free, free to do as his conscience commands him. Mrs. Boswell, who had no liking for her husband's gruff and burly friend Dr. Johnson, and who thought the philosopher had far too much influence over Mr. Boswell, once said "she had very often seen a bear led about by a man, but never before had she seen a man led about by a bear;" but every man is who lets the brutal part of himself or of other men dictate to him, every man is who allows any sensuous indulgence to lead him where his conscience tells him he ought not go. A man led about by a bear is not our idea of a strong man. Manhood, the world is slowly coming to see, lies not in physical or intellectual qualities, but in moral dispositions. Both a giant and a philosopher may be brutes, but he who is strong in truth, in honor, in purity, in self-culture, in the right, in the Lord, is a strong man.

Like the lower forms, such strength is acquired, and by the same methods. Whoever wishes to be an athlete or a scholar must consent to deny himself some very pleasant things. You must go into training to be an athlete, you must go to school to be a scholar; and in each instance self-indulgence is forbidden. There must be no dainty dishes, no stimulating beverages or narcotics for the athlete; no midnight amusements, no morning hours wasted in sleep, for the scholar. Just so far as each is in earnest there is a positive delight in any self-denial that offers an increased probability of success. Let the athlete or scholar be worthy of the name, and he stops at nothing that will apparently bring him a little nearer what he wishes to be. He sees no attractiveness in anything that would weaken him and his chances of success. Nothing more than this is asked of those who wish for character, moral strength. Self-denial stares them in the face the moment they begin their quest, but it is the denial of that self which can be strengthened only at the expense of the very self they are anxious to develop. Like the athlete and the scholar, the man must avoid every indulgence, every amusement even, that saps and undermines those fine virtues that must all be preserved and developed if he is ever to fill his own idea of the strong man. To be anything you must deny some part of yourself. To be a man you have only to deny that part of yourself which is unworthy of you. There is no more self-denial for those who are seeking to be strong in the Lord than there is for those who are seeking any other kind of strength; only it is a different kind of self-denial.

But no man ever gets strength of any sort whatever by simply not doing some things. What he gives up is the mere clearing the ground of weeds, so that the crop he wishes to raise can have a fair chance. There are negative Christians, or imitations called such, whose only claim to be strong is that they have given up everything that makes men weak. They permit themselves no self-indulgences, no pernicious amusements; they do nothing that could sap their strength. But what are they doing to increase it? Where is the athlete or scholar that wins prizes simply by not doing injurious things? Muscle and brain must be fed and exercised if they are ever to be strong; so must the soul. Some men are by nature morally as well as physically and intellectually stronger than others, but no man ever yet had a strong character that was not made strong by his own efforts. He nourished and exercised himself with that end in view. When he found that the moral giants had all fed their souls on the moral truths of the Bible, he considered this good evidence that there must be something in this book especially adapted for strengthening the conscience and the soul of man. Must a young man or a young woman read the Bible? Not necessarily merely to be what many young men and young women are; but for those who wish to be morally and spiritually strong this is the one indispensable book. Even men like Mr. Huxley, who are not willing to concede its divine character, yet place the Bible above all other books as a moral force. They do not see, they confess, how, without the use of it, ideals so lofty and inspirations so potent can ever be produced. When you are told to read the Bible, you need not think of yourself as going around with a flexible-covered copy of the sacred volume under your arm, questioning all your friends as to the meaning of various passages in the minor prophets and in Revelation. I have nothing to say against carrying a Bible under your arm, but the place where it will do you the most good to carry it is where Coligny and Cromwell and Havelock and Livingstone carried theirs: in the heart.

But the Bible itself urges those who feel their need of wisdom and strength to ask for what they want of Him who moved holy men of old to write these words. It is a book that draws attention to itself only that it may fix the attention thus secured upon an ever-living Being. Must a young person pray? There is something natural about reading anything, even the Bible; but this bowing like a carved figure in an unaccustomed attitude, and muttering words in the air—what relation can there be between such an exercise and the practical questions that are impatiently waiting the conclusion of these orisons? This wise book constantly associates worship and conduct. "They that wait upon the Lord shall renew their strength." Strong men like Coligny and Cromwell and Havelock and Livingstone believed that they could not fight their battles successfully without prayer. They did not lay great stress upon a particular attitude, or upon any set forms, or upon words at all. Prayer, to them, was not a mere religious ceremony working as incantations are supposed to work: it was direct communication with the one Being in this universe whose power is always making for righteousness, and who is always eager to help those who feel themselves sinking. So to think of prayer is to change the obligation into a privilege, and on the use we make of it will depend, to an extent which probably very few of us realize, our efficiency as moral forces.

From some points of view this seems to be rather an unfortunate time to begin life. All the professions and all forms of business, they tell us, are overcrowded. The supply everywhere seems greater than the demand, and many of you, perhaps, have already had the sense of being superfluous. But the world is by no means overstocked with young men and women who are strong in moral purpose, strong in character, strong in the Lord. There is no profession or business that will not hasten to make room for any number of such young persons as soon as their presence is known. All the large firms of our own and of every other city have unsatisfactory employés whom they would be glad to weed out if they could be certain of filling the vacancies with trustworthy persons. All the professions have a number of places reserved and kept unoccupied, waiting, not for candidates—there are scores of applicants for each—but waiting till the right man appears, and then immediately the call for his services will be ready. The political world, swarming as it is with a hungry hoard, is in greatest need of strong young men, young men whose back-bones are not to be bent though a whole party try its hand at it; young men whose knees will not bow to the tyrant's cap though obloquy and obscurity are threatened; young men who will dare, as young men did fifty years ago, to lift their voices and cry out against iniquity, though entrenched behind majorities, respectability and religion. For such young men there is plenty of room in the political world, and wherever they are will be the top.

Society, too, has places for more than four hundred

young persons of this sort. They may not be welcomed with any great enthusiasm by those who are already in; they will be looked upon, possibly, as interloping puritans; but the sincerity of grateful recognition on the part of the few will more than compensate for the indifference or the recoil of the many. In every social stratum there are some who set themselves determinedly against excesses, against degrading self-indulgence, against frivolity and materialism. They are lonely; they feel themselves in a hopeless minority. If you can bring them a reinforcement of moral strength, you will be as welcome as Blücher was to Wellington, as La Fayette was to Washington. If you have nothing of this kind to bring, if you are a vacillating person with no strong moral purpose, if everything that is pleasant seems to you desirable without any question of right, then society of any sort will be fatal to you, and you will do what you can to be fatal to it.

What the business and professional and political and social worlds want is, as Canon Farrar says, "not echoes, but voices." It may not be yours to choose to be a voice that shall startle any of these worlds and force them to give heed to you as to a modern prophet, but it is yours to choose whether you will supinely echo the belittling sentiments that fill the air, or whether you will lift your voice and strike with some truth that is in your heart straight through the soft, enervating harmonies that lull the senses into ignoble slumber. You are not strong enough, no young man or woman is, to be such a voice till you have gained strength of character and moral purpose from the Lord.

When Paul recounted all the parts of the complex armor that he thought necessary for those who have the high purpose of resisting all the powers that make for unrighteousness, he had no desire to frighten them or us into unnecessary caution or excessive equipment. We are all tempted at times to do this, and we do not always successfully resist the temptation. We half-unconsciously exaggerate dangers to heighten the value of our suggestions as to the way of avoiding them. Paul has not yielded to any such temptation here if he ever felt it. He has given us a highly figurative, but not overwrought, description of what we have to contend with, and of the need there is, therefore, to be forearmed. His soldier, when he has him entirely accoutred with his girdle and breastplate and sandals and shield and helmet and sword, impresses us as somewhat overweighted, and as liable to be hindered, if not crushed, by his weapons, offensive and defensive; but try this armament for the next few days and see if you cannot carry it easily. A girdle of truth, a breastplate of righteousness, a shield of faith, a helmet of salvation and a sword of the Spirit can all be used without impediment and without ostentation. Any lighter equipment than that in the conflict in which we must take part will prove wholly inadequate.

Be strong, not as the brutes, not as the unthinking machine, but as men. Be strong to resist wrong and to beat it down. To this Christ calls you. It is a call to warfare, yet to peace. "Nothing can bring you peace," Emerson says, "but the triumph of principles;" and it is to that triumph Christ is pledged to lead those who follow him. It is a call to run a hard race on a pathway beset by dangers, but arched with flowers and palms of victory. Running swiftly and courageously, many a sweet blossom and green palm will be shaken down to gladden us by the way, and the pulse will be quickened, and hope will be high, and the joy and safety of strength will be to us delightful antepasts of the unspeakable awards that await the victors when at last the goal shall be reached.

X.
SUCCESS.

X.

SUCCESS.

"His Lord said unto him, Well done, thou good and faithful servant."—MATT. xxv. 21.

THERE was room enough in the Roman Pantheon for any god who had worshipers sufficiently enthusiastic to claim a place for him there, and there is room enough in the world's temple of success for a pillar or a tablet to any claimant who can muster a sufficiently enthusiastic crowd of admirers. No questions are asked as to the cause of that enthusiasm: it may have been excited by rare ability in numbering stars or in counting votes, in helping one's fellow-men or one's party and one's self. Here in this modern pantheon are altars equally magnificent to men who have given away large fortunes honestly made, and to men who have dishonestly appropriated fortunes quite as large for their own use. There stands a pillar to keep alive the memory of a martyr whose death meant life for a whole community, and by its side is a pillar of the same sort to a manipulator whose life meant death to banks and railroads, and to every financial enterprise upon which he could lay his wrecking hand.

That there should be some confusion in the minds of those who stroll through this temple is inevitable. The natural inference for any one would be that success and notoriety are synonymous, and that to become notorious, in whatever way, is the thing to be sought. This is not only the natural, but the ordinary and actual, inference of those who are forming their ideas of success from what they see in this temple. We must do something, they are saying to themselves, to push our way through the crowd and force attention: it makes very little difference what. If you can write a book or paint a picture or discover a new force or some unsuspected utility in an old one, if you can pierce an unknown continent or the ice of the polar sea or so play upon the curiosity and credulity of men as to fix their expectations and their hopes upon yourself, you have solved the problem, and may take your place among the select company of successful men.

> "All the proud virtue of this vaunting world
> Fawns on success, howe'er acquired."

There is something quite clear and understandable about success so defined and achieved. The prize to be sought is plainly in sight, and so is the road that leads to it. So long as we can forget the heights that are above us and the depths that are within us it is possible to believe that success of this sort will be eminently satisfactory, but the moment these heights and depths come into view, doubts of a very serious sort will be begotten. How can we consider the problem solved when factors so important as these heights and depths are left out altogether? One glance inward upon a man's own soul with its throng of aspirations wholly untouched by notoriety is enough to make all but the intoxicated question the correctness of the world's definition of success. Was it right to sacrifice a hundred yearnings, confessedly of the nobler sort, to a single desire acknowledgedly so common as easily to become vulgar? Was it wise to barter truth and sincerity and purity and honor, and probably health and culture, for a notoriety from which all that is still left of manhood shrinks unsatisfied and disappointed away?

If a glance inward can beget such doubts, what vitality will be given them by a glance upward! Those silent stars, a few nights hence it may be, are to look down upon our graves; what matter then about pillars of marble and tablets of brass in the temple of Fame? Was it worth while to pay so dearly for a possession that could be held so briefly? The element of time is a large element of value. No man would pay as much for an ice-palace as for the same edifice in stone, or for a memorial arch in wood as for its *fac-simile* in marble. Gold and diamonds have no value on a sinking ship; any one who likes can have them for the few seconds before the final plunge. This notoriety that the world wishes to foist on us as genuine success can last us, it is admitted, for only a little while, and then, as the silent stars seem to forewarn us, the cheers upon which we have lived will be as silent as are these planets that have looked down upon thousands of generations that have wasted their foolish lives for just such evanescent huzzahs. Their silence suggests something more than this. "Beyond us," they seem to say, for so men, almost in spite of themselves, have interpreted their silence, "is a spirit-world whose population is every moment augmented by those who once dwelt upon your earth." Who are they that are accounted successful in the abodes of eternity? We can answer in part the question for ourselves. Think this generation out of this world into that, and then ask yourself how many of those you have been accustomed to call successful men here appear to you now to be so there. The winners of a great fortune or a great name or a great position shrivel under that test. The distinctions upon which they assumed and were conceded a superiority among their fellow-men you feel have disappeared altogether.

Your own heart will have prepared you to anticipate some such words from Him who is to be the Judge in the final apportionment of awards as those Christ speaks to his disciples when he describes the last great assize in his parable. The "Well done" that sounds in the ears of those who have been really successful is not heard at all by those who have aimed for notoriety in whatever way, but by those who have aimed for fidelity. The first requisite for success, then, according to Christ's idea of it, is to give up all thought of it. As Jeremiah said to Baruch, "Seekest thou great things for thyself? Seek them not." As Christ said to his disciples, "He that would be greatest among you, let him be your minister," let him be most efficient in service, let him do most in carrying his fellow-men to a higher plane. He substitutes, it has been said, "the greatness of love for the love of greatness." This idea of success and that of the world are the complete antitheses of each other. The world knows nothing about any success that has not attained extraordinary and noteworthy results of some sort. If such results are forthcoming, it is entirely indifferent as to the means employed. Christ has nothing whatever to say about noteworthy results: his successful man is one who has been wholly engrossed in the commonplace occupation of doing the best he can with commissions, small or great, given him by his Master. In Christ's eyes means and motives overshadow results altogether. Each of those who received his "Well done" was one whose only purpose was to do well; and that purpose, whatever comes of it, makes a man, according to Christ's ideas, successful.

There can be nothing accidental or involuntary about success of this sort. Prominence, notoriety, may be matters of birth or of good-fortune. The world's successful man may have done nothing himself to win the prize; it may have dropped into his hands while he was almost asleep, with only consciousness enough to close his fingers upon his luck; but fidelity is never hereditary or accidental. With a great effort he who has it has turned away from all lower ambitions, and with a mighty movement of soul has chosen this as the supreme passion of his life. And as no chance can bring success of this sort, so no chance can prevent it. Nothing is more certain than that prominence and notoriety are very often denied to those who would seem to have merited them, else Addison would never have written,

> "It is not in mortals to command success,
> But we'll do more, Sempronius: we'll deserve it."

Notoriety is lawless and fickle. Those who have deserved to win her may for some inexplicable reason fail altogether, while she flings herself almost unsought into the arms of the unworthy. But success, as Christ defined it, is as intangible to chance as the earth's orbit. Nay, nothing in the physical world can be half so assured as this, for God himself must change before fidelity can fail of his "Well done."

This brings success easily within reach of us all. Prominence and notoriety must, in the very nature of the case, be confined to a few. The moment you lift the Vale of Interlaken to the level of the Jungfrau your mountain has disappeared. To give prominence and notoriety to every one would be to rob the few of it who once towered above their fellow-men. It is this that has awakened the murderous envy and hatred of men. The prizes they were after were not half numerous enough to go around. There was only one, perhaps, for ten or a hundred thousand competitors, and every one of these hundreds or thousands looked upon every other one in the same class as an enemy, and was right. Every eye was full of envy and every heart of hate, and there was no help for it. But Christ's idea of success changes all these conditions. To make room higher up some one else must be crowded out of the way or be gotten rid of, but there are plenty of places lower down, the best places for service, where Christ wants his disciples to go, and where just in proportion to their fidelity they will be found, and their success will be exactly commensurate with their faithfulness.

There is no need for any one who is willing to adopt Christ's view of things to look anxiously or eagerly for openings that may lead to success. Turn which way you will, such doors stand wide open. Emerson thinks that the parlor and the college and the counting-room demand as much courage as the sea or the camp, if that might possibly be considered an open question, it certainly is not, that the parlor and the college and counting-room, and the mill and the shop and the kitchen included, demand as much fidelity as the sea or the camp, and are as good fields for its exercise. The field is a matter of very little if any consequence in Christ's eyes: it is the fidelity that is shown in it. He states in so many words that the final award will be accompanied by great surprises, that many judged by the world and the Church to have made prime successes will be given low places, if any at all, and many who were thought little of in the world and the Church will be advanced to the head, for they have been most faithful, perhaps in most confined and uninspiring fields. Paul's anticipations of receiving a crown in that day were not based upon any of the results of his work, upon the number of churches established or converts made, but he was certain of the reward, because he had fought the good fight; and the certainty he felt for himself he felt for every one else who had done the same, though what the world, and even these faithful ones, would call a victory may never have been won.

Still, though we may accept Christ's ideas of success as heartily as it is possible for beings as short-sighted as ourselves to do, there will be a longing, more or less marked according to our temperament and the degree of our faith, for results. Believe as we may, and as we must if we are Christians, that fidelity is the essence of success, and that results are only its accidents, we cannot prevent ourselves from having strong desires for those accidents. Very possibly we should not attempt to destroy, but only to control, such desires;

for results will ordinarily follow fidelity, and, while they are not to be sought as ends in themselves, they are not to be undervalued when they are the ripened fruits of fidelity. While Christ commends the faithfulness of the good servants in the parable, and while we feel confident he would have commended any one of them as heartily who had done his best to invest and increase his talents, even if he had been unfortunate, and in putting the money out to the exchangers had lost it all, yet it seems fair to draw the inference that in real life desired results will in the great majority of instances follow fidelity, as in the parable the increase of the talents follows the conscientious care of them.

That the man who is intensely anxious to be faithful rather than excitedly eager for results is in the best condition to command such results is almost self-evident. He will have the two qualities that all the world agrees in naming as requisite for the production of results in a marked degree, industry and tenacity of purpose. Fidelity and industry, while not synonymous, are indissoluble. They are like the two brothers bound by a vital ligament upon which the touch of the separating knife meant death to both. Men have "toiled terribly" for glory and wealth, and even for pleasure; but other men have been as ambitious and avaricious and sensuous, yet never to the point of industry. Some other avenue has seemed to open up to what they wished, and they have eagerly chosen it; but the faithful man has but one hope. For him there is no other possible approach to the object of his desires. Great students of human nature have felt that they were safest in making their appeal to this sense of fidelity, of duty. Both Wellington and Nelson had little to say to their soldiers and sailors about glory or rich prizes or the delights of captured capitals: they had much to say about duty and what they had a right to expect from faithful servants of their king and country. Fidelity is the only motive to industry that has no let up in it. The man who toils terribly for glory or power or pleasure when he gets what he has toiled for finds the mainspring of his energies is broken, and he falls supinely upon the prize he has won; but the man who is toiling that he may be faithful to the trust committed to him will be urged on till life itself is over and his account rendered. What is to prevent such industry from producing results often of the most brilliant sort?

The other requisite, the world says, for marked efficiency in attaining the end desired is tenacity of purpose. But who is he that is most calmly tenacious of his purpose? Is it the man who has vowed the great vow to himself and the silent Fates that he will be prominent and notorious? Can such a man be calm when he thinks of the tremendous difficulties he must surmount and the awful uncertainties that will still hover about him even after these obstacles are over-passed? Can a man's heart beat regularly when his fate hangs on the throwing of a dice? Or can such a man choose his path and hold to it tenaciously when short cuts are constantly coming in sight and a tumult of voices urges him to take these or direful consequences? The man has yet to appear with a purpose tenacious enough to resist these temptations to forsake the road originally chosen. From Cæsar to Napoleon I. and from Napoleon III. to Boulanger the short cut taken against the man's own better judgment has proved fatal. It must always be so; whoever lives for results must be ready to change his route whenever some other seems more direct. While the end sought may be always the same, the man will vacillate and move uneasily hither and thither as he hurries impatiently toward it.

What a contrast to all this is the steady, unswerving tread of the man who is striving for fidelity, without reference to results! There can be for him no alluring short cuts. He may, of course, be tempted to unfaithfulness, but he cannot be tempted with the hope of ever reaching what he seeks by any other except the straight path. His reliance must always be in doing well what he has to do, while the reliance of the man whose eye is on results will be in getting something to do where noise and bluster can be substituted for sweat and skill. So every path to-day is crowded, not with men of industry and purpose, but with men who are hurrying from place to place with the hope that by some lucky chance they may some time find something that will yield results without effort. Those musicians on our street-corners who play with the aid of a few well-arranged wires a half dozen instruments at a time, and, though they never can make any music on any of them, yet attract much attention, are the embodiment of the popular craze for doing any number of things, however poorly, if a momentary prominence may be gained by it. Such a mountebank any man, whatever his gifts, may become who makes the producing of results the purpose of his life.

As I draw near the end of this series of discourses to the young I find myself eager as friends are when time hurries apace and they must part to speak some word that might linger with you, some helpful word that would be in itself an inspiration in the sore struggle of life. I can find no other with more of destiny in it than this we have heard Christ repeating to us to-night: "Fidelity." Fling away all thought of prominence or of notoriety. "'Tis only noble to be good." Be true to God, to Christ, whatever comes, and your fidelity will achieve all fitting results. "Seek ye first," he says to you, "the kingdom of God and his righteousness, and all these things shall be added unto you." Whatever else fails you, you shall assuredly have at last the evidence of your eternal success in his "Well done, good and faithful servant!"

THE END.

www.ingramcontent.com/pod-product-compliance
Lightning Source LLC
Chambersburg PA
CBHW030307170426
43202CB00009B/899